P9-CKX-221

POETRY AND THE MODERN WORLD

A STUDY OF POETRY IN ENGLAND
BETWEEN 1900 AND 1939

*

BY DAVID DAICHES

OCTAGON BOOKS

A DIVISION OF FARRAR, STRAUS AND GIROUX

New York   1978

Copyright 1940 by the University of Chicago

Reprinted 1978

OCTAGON BOOKS
A DIVISION OF FARRAR, STRAUS & GIROUX, INC.
19 Union Square West
New York, N.Y. 10003

Library of Congress Cataloging in Publication Data

Daiches, David, 1912-
    Poetry and the modern world.

        Reprint of the ed. published by University of Chicago Press, Chicago.
        Includes bibliographical references and index.
        1. English poetry—20th century—History and criticism.   I. Title.
[PR610.D25   1978]   821'.9'1209   78-15333
ISBN 0-374-92026-5

Manufactured by Braun-Brumfield, Inc.
Ann Arbor, Michigan
Printed in the United States of America

TO MY BROTHER
LIONEL HENRY DAICHES

*

Here in the heat, an unco way frae hame,
I'm dowie wi' remembering, like a fool,
Lang syne when we were daft an' young an' skeigh,
Crossing the Meedies on the way tae school.

Ye'll mind the grannies in the rocks at Crail,
The nichts we spun for mackerel oot-by Kyle,
Or—later—at the Royal or Rutherford's,
In guid auld style.

Aye, we hae scrambled on the Pentland Hills,
We've reared Dunsappie tadpoles in a jar:
Cockenzie folk hae seen us lingering late
By the pools where the muckle partans are.

Och, man, the nicht at Stirling we were fou!
Yon time we crossed Strome Ferry at peep o' the sun!
An' noo ye're a sodger and I—dinna laugh—a professor,
An' oor wark's no done.

Aye man, it's a lang fareweel tae the auld daft days,
The lichts hae gone oot on the shore an' we canna see.
Scunnersome things are scrauchin' in oor puir warl',
An' they're lookin' for you an' me.

Here in the heat, an unco way frae hame,
I toast the yesterdays that time has torn,
An' when Auld Reekie's lichts shine clear again
We'll drink thegither tae the morn's morn.

CHICAGO
July 1940

FOREWORD

I HAVE endeavored in the following pages to present certain aspects of modern English poetry and to discuss them in such a way as to throw some new light on poetic activity in the first forty years of the present century. This work is intended not as a complete history of English poetry during the period but rather as a series of what I hope are suggestive studies. I am well aware that I have omitted to mention many poets of ability: I have written only about those whom I felt able to discuss with some originality, and where I had nothing that I thought new or significant to say I have said nothing.

I claim no finality for my views. It seems to me important—and more important than ever these days—that a level of intelligent discourse about literature should be maintained. There is no single way to an understanding of the complex phenomena of culture; but, if those who are interested talk to each other reasonably and with intelligence, we shall gradually learn more about these important matters. I should like to think of my work as a modest contribution to a symposium.

Acknowledgment is due to *Poetry: A Magazine of Verse* for permission to reprint parts of an essay on W. H. Auden which first appeared there.

D. D.

TABLE OF CONTENTS

I

THE LEGACY OF VICTORIANISM: POETRY AT THE
END OF THE NINETEENTH CENTURY

Page 1

II

THOMAS HARDY—A. E. HOUSMAN—GERARD
MANLEY HOPKINS

Page 17

III

GEORGIAN POETRY

Page 38

IV

WAR POETRY—THE IMAGISTS—POST-WAR SATIRE—
THE SITWELLS

Page 61

V

T. E. HULME AND T. S. ELIOT

Page 90

VI

T. S. ELIOT

Page 106

IX

TABLE OF CONTENTS

VII

W. B. YEATS—I

Page 128

VIII

W. B. YEATS—II

Page 156

IX

POETRY IN THE 1930's—I: CECIL DAY LEWIS

Page 190

X

POETRY IN THE 1930's—II: W. H. AUDEN AND
STEPHEN SPENDER

Page 214

EPILOGUE

Page 240

INDEX

Page 243

CHAPTER I

THE LEGACY OF VICTORIANISM: POETRY AT THE END OF THE NINETEENTH CENTURY

O N SEPTEMBER 3, 1939, Stephen Spender, the English poet and critic, wrote these words in the journal which he began on that critical day:

I feel as if I could not write again. Words seem to break in my mind like sticks when I put them down on paper. I cannot see how to spell some of them. Sentences are covered with leaves, and I really cannot see the line of the branch that carries the green meanings.

The crisis involved more than Spender's feeling that he could not write again, and more than the politicians of London, Paris, and Berlin suspected as they faced the beginning of the second World War. A cycle in the history of English culture had, for good or ill, been completed, and Spender's admission of his inability to write was symbolic. And in the realm of literature, the movements which began with what might loosely be called the rejection of the Tennysonian tradition in poetry had concluded with the disappearance from under the poets' feet of the ground on which they had based themselves in their gestures of protest, escape, or revolution. There had been many and violent changes in the English poetic attitude between Wordsworth and Yeats, between Shelley and Wystan Auden, of which the most violent had come toward the beginning of the present century; there was the flow toward

1

the Tennysonian tradition and the ebb from it, but it was the ebb and flow of the same tide. The two factors concerned were the Poet and the World, and the great change involved the way the poet regarded his place in the world, his attitude toward it, his duty to it, and his way of expressing that attitude and that duty. But, in essentials, the world remained constant. The shift involved beliefs, not the objective situation. But on September 3, 1939, it looked as though for the first time for over a century and a half there was to be a major change in the objective situation as well as in the poets' attitude. Whatever the future might bring, it seemed certain that, when the smoke had cleared away, the poet would be faced with the problem not of defining and expressing new attitudes toward a familiar situation but of adjusting himself to a new state of affairs. Whether that is to mean a rebirth of poetry of the kind that followed the accession of the Tudors at the conclusion of the Wars of the Roses, or a cessation of it of the kind brought by the collapse of the Roman Empire, we cannot yet tell. But when the smoke screen of the future lies thickest is the time to clarify and understand the past.

What has been happening to poetry in Great Britain in the first forty years of the twentieth century? There were many movements and countermovements in that brief period of history, for poetry (unlike fiction, which, because of its sheer size and the time it takes to write a novel, is less responsive) reacts easily and speedily to every slight change in the intellectual climate of the time. Poetry and, to a lesser degree, painting are the most responsive of the arts: they mirror changing attitudes in much greater detail than sculpture or fiction, for to write a poem may be the work of only a few hours. And with the decline of the long poem in the twentieth century this becomes the general rule in poetry.

The result is that to trace a pattern in the poetry of even forty years is not an easy task. It is comparatively easy to write a factual chronological survey or a series of individual essays on separate works, but to try to put the material into some shape, to find out its relation to the social and intellectual background, to see movements for what they are and in their right proportions, is a task which one might be deemed presumptuous or foolish to attempt. It is being attempted here not because the author can claim any completeness or finality for his analysis but simply in the conviction that an honest endeavor to see the recent past clearly and justly can never be totally without value, and that, since in any case each age must write its own history of the past, an account of post-Victorian English poetry up to the outbreak of the present war in Europe, made just when that period has reached its close, will have a peculiar interest of its own. It is meant as the first, not the last, word on the subject.

If we were asked to say what general shift in attitude took place when the Victorian era gave way to the modern, we might answer that, in very general terms, the shift was from an attitude which, in various ways (ranging from total acquiescence to prophetic denunciation), recognized the responsibility of the poet to the world in which he found himself to an attitude which rejected that responsibility (the rejection ranging from simple escape to the attempt to replace the rejected world by a new one). By and large, the nineteenth- and the twentieth-century poets were concerned with the same world. With the growth of industrialism and other more specific features of the modern world there were important changes in the proportion of one part of that world to others, but in general the world of Auden is that of Wordsworth—a world of town and country, of city slum and poor peasant, of businessman, professional and worker, of rich and poor, of conservative and radical, of cynic and idealist, of oppressor and oppressed. That is, the world as objective situation remained, in its general shape, more or less the same: it developed, but not out of recognition. But the world in its capacity for arousing hope or despair, courage or fear, optimism or pessimism, changed a great deal. The condemned man's final meal before the gallows, objectively considered, may be very similar to his previous meals; but it is very different to him.

The modern poet, then—using the term to denote the poets of the first forty years of the present century— tends to be·concerned with gestures of rejection and can on the whole be opposed to the poet of the Victorian tradition, whose gestures were mainly of acceptance. The aim of Tennyson, as he saw it, was to come to terms with his age: he may not have achieved his aim completely or comfortably, but there can be little doubt that it *was* his aim, as it was Browning's. The optimism of Browning and the pessimism of Tennyson (for taken as a whole *In Memoriam* is pessimistic) are both products of this aim: the former tried to achieve it by breeziness and ruggedness, the latter by

4

worry, morality, and (alternatively) choicely cadenced hysteria. The revival of dramatic poetry by both these poets represented a sort of compass split which (as in Donne's famous simile) sent one leg off into other consciousnesses or other periods of history while the other leg remained, as it were, in Queen Victoria's London,

> As though it in the center sit,
> Yet when the other far doth rome,
> It leans and hearkens after it. . . . .

In Tennyson's best work we often find that, to borrow Professor Elton's phrase describing *Tithonus*, "all is beauty and *desiderium*." It is the expansive, yet plangent, aestheticism of a poet who indulges his emotions from within a rather stuffy Victorian interior. In such an environment the search for beauty is bound to be accompanied by either nostalgia or bravado, and the elegiac quality of Tennyson's lyrics is the result of the former, while a great deal of Browning's subject matter and technique is the result of the latter.

The dramatic poems of Browning suggest a man leaving home because he is not sure that the peace he has made with his family will stand the strain of his presence: Browning's choice of curious characters and curious times (we think of Bishop Blougram, the grammarian, Fra Lippo Lippi, and the duke who displayed the portrait of his last duchess) arose, it would seem, from his desire not to put his acceptance of the Victorian world to too great a test. He was not what modern critics are fond of calling an "escapist," for he was only too willing to come to terms with the life of his day; yet he made his terms with a casualness, a breeziness, which suggests that he would not have liked to look too closely at the world with which he had agreed to be at peace, and this suggestion is borne out by his choice of subjects.

Browning went through the motions of acceptance rather too light-heartedly, but he accepted the Victorian world nonetheless. Tennyson is more seriously representative of the poet of his age, because he took his duty toward it more seriously and was really bothered about basing his acceptance of nineteenth-century English civilization on some sort of philosophical synthesis. He is too often regarded as merely the thoughtless echo of Victorian mores. This is unjust: he struggled hard in order to become that echo, and if in the end he reached the same position as that which Mrs. Grundy and some others had held all along, the tragedy lies in the object of his quest, not in the manner in which he pursued it.

Matthew Arnold demonstrated his sense of responsibility to his own age with considerable vigor, though in his prose rather than in his poetry. After the 1860's he practically ceased to write poetry and turned to the problem of improving his countrymen. He neither rejected his age nor desired a revolution; he simply tried to educate it. His poetry has the pleasing and thoughtful melancholy of a sensitive Oxford don indulging his sense of beauty and of *lacrimae rerum* before leaving the city of dreaming spires in order to do something about adult education in industrial towns. For all his denunciation he, too, accepted his age: a desire to improve is one of the most convincing gestures of acceptance.

As for Rossetti and the Pre-Raphaelites, we must remember that Victorianism had its stained-glass aspect and that both Queen Victoria and Mrs. Grundy would have approved of the Blessed Damozel—so long as she remained in Heaven. Rossetti played around with great skill and very genuine poetic ability in the less obvious of those fields which the Victorians were quite willing to lease to Art for its legitimate gambols. Passion and old romance, witchcraft and balladry, religious symbols and primitive simplicity—these implied no rejection of the Victorian age but were simply "Art" in its alloted place. Rossetti was a greater genius than is generally admitted, and he did a better job than any other poet of his age in exploiting poetically types of experience which did not involve him (as Tennyson's did) in the more obvious and dated aspects of Victorianism. Yet he was neither rebel nor escapist but a great poet who sublimated into fine poetry tendencies in the civilization of his time which emerged in the hands of less genuine artists as sham gothic and sundry types of eyewash.

William Morris is the first important poet of the nineteenth century in whom the desire to educate and change his fellow-men reaches proportions where it becomes something very like rejection of his age and all that it stood for. Yet that rejection is hardly if at all apparent in his poetry. He ranges from the pallidness of Rossetti at his worst to the violence of Browning at his best, as a comparison of *The Earthly Paradise* with a short poem like "The Haystack in the Floods" will immediately show. At times he is sedately frolicking in the legitimate "field of the cloth of gold" which the Victorians kept free (and nicely fenced round) for artists, and at times he is doing what Browning did when he took lush and decadent characters from late Renaissance times and made them meditate or shout. But at all times there is a disparity between Morris the poet and Morris the man; and the split personality is suggestive. Morris the man tended to reject his age quite vigorously, while Morris the poet wavered between several types of gesture, all of which were basically gestures of acceptance, however indirectly so. His life and work mark a crumbling and a transition.

Then there is Algernon Charles Swinburne, whose feverish if skilful gestures of rejection peter out in sheer virtuosity and sometimes not even in that. He is an important symptom and demonstrates that by now the poet could find little nourishment in the life of his time. From now on renunciation, rejection, and escape are the commonest attitudes among the poets: escape into words and a doctrine of the functionlessness of art, renunciation in the form of mysticism, aestheticism, or "private" art, rejection as pessimism or rebellion.

There were, of course, other tendencies. Those poets who were able to go behind the modern world in allegiance to an older tradition which for them was still vital and significant often produced interesting and skilful minor poetry—minor because, among other reasons, the whole basis of their inspiration was an attitude largely outside the historical development of English culture. Coventry Patmore, who had real genius, was an eccentric in a sense that even Oscar Wilde was not: his work represented neither an attempt to come to terms with his age nor a rejection of it as a result of its inadequacies becoming apparent. He goes to an older, Catholic, tradition, and when he does criticize his age he does so in the terms of that tradition, not out of any awareness of the necessities of the times. He regards the increase of the franchise achieved in 1867 as "the great crime" perpetrated by "the false English Nobles and their Jew,"[1] and such a view of Disraeli's Reform Bill shows clearly how removed from contemporary realities and tendencies his attitude was. His political attitude is not, of course, important, but it illustrates that he was operating in what was by this time a backwater of English civilization. There is a lot to be said for what we might call "backwater poets" of culture. They often have greater integrity, and see their vision more clearly, than writers who make too facile gestures toward the spirit of the age. Coventry Patmore, Francis Thompson, and Alice Meynell all possess qualities not only of poetic skill of a high order but of genuineness and passion. These three Catholic poets with their sincere faith and intense feeling remain interesting outsiders, with a few followers (in some degree) among the Georgian poets—indeed, Alice Meynell, born in 1847, lived until 1922 and published volumes of poetry throughout the war years and later. They are to be distinguished alike from "escapists" and rebels, yet in attitude at least they are not of their time; history was not on their side, and the tradition they represented remained of the past, with personal validity for some but without real relevance to the sweep of English cultural history from the Victorian into the modern world.

[1] And defended his view in a letter to Gerard Manley Hopkins (*Further Letters of Gerard Manley Hopkins*, ed. C. C. Abbott [London, 1938], p. 197). Hopkins himself, the most impressive of the Catholic poets, receives separate consideration in a later chapter.

In any attempt to sum up briefly the nineteenth-century traditions in English poetry as a preliminary to discussing the twentieth, we must be content to pick out a few representative names and use them as symbols or as pegs on which to hang an argument. The popular mind is not misleading here: the present-day reader who thinks of Tennyson as the personal representative of Queen Victoria and what she stood for is recognizing, though in too crude a form, a fundamental truth. And the view of the poets of the nineties that regards them as hysterical fugitives seeking any way out of the stuffy Palace of Art that Tennyson and his minor followers had come to inhabit rather than remain there to suffocate has a great deal of truth as applied to the somewhat vaguely defined "aesthetic" groups of that period. But these groups are neither homogeneous nor easy to understand. Do they represent the fag end of the Tennysonian tradition, or the Swinburnian revolt stuttering toward its final extinction, or the rejection of contemporary life as any sort of basis for art (thus being predecessors of the political rebels among the poets of our own time)? Some inquiry into their attitudes and techniques is necessary before their place can be properly understood either in itself or historically. It is too easy to see them as a sort of *fin de siècle* disease preceding the death of the nineteenth century. But this is to be fooled by the arbitrary divisions of chronology: some more substantial diagnosis is required.

The theory which seems to flit behind the practice of those poets of the nineties who were influenced both by the Pre-Raphaelites and by the French "art for

art's sake" poets is that personal sensation is at once
the origin and the aim of poetry, because (though this
further proposition is only doubtfully implied) to seek
for any other kind of value is to implicate the poet in
a world which has no genuine interest in art however
defined, a world which it is therefore the poet's duty
to despise and, on occasion, to shock. Actually, nearly
all of these poets did have positive values, however ill
defined, which their aesthetic theories denied. Their
denial of these values was simply a way of declaring
their distrust of certain contemporary attitudes which
had no validity for them; but the very fact that they
felt this distrust meant that they believed in certain
countervalues. Some found these countervalues in
Catholicism, embraced for its ability to yield a basis
for types of emotional experience denied by the normal
middle-class way of life and of thought. Yet it was less
a belief in Catholic theology than a desire to find a
sanction for what might be called their nonbourgeois
emotions that led them to religion. Francis Thompson
and Alice Meynell adhered genuinely to the faith, but
the conversion of Lionel Johnson, Aubrey Beardsley,
and Ernest Dowson was symbolic rather than real.
What they were really seeking was a certain freedom
and spontaneity of the emotional life that both the conscious and the unconscious mind of late Victorian England denied. It denied it consciously in the Bentham-
ite-cum-Darwinian view that it held, a view which
combined the older utilitarianism and the more recent
evolutionary ideas in the service of the capitalist way
of life: it denied it unconsciously in the place it rele-
gated to the artist in society.

11

For what, after all, was the place which the great Victorian middle class had assigned to the artist? It was not a single one. The artist was regarded alternatively as purveyor of "uplift" or licensed clown. Of these functions, that of purveyor of uplift was the more dignified, but at the same time more cramping. Wordsworth by starting as a prophet had ended as a trite schoolteacher, and the awful warning was grimly underlined in the practice of innumerable writers of magazine verse, which the modern critic who wants to understand just how the general reading public regarded poetry and its function would do well to look into. The more sensitive poets thus recoiled from the prophetic or "vatic" view of their function, partly because accepting it in their time meant risking descent from Mount Sinai to the girls' school, and partly because the countervalues which they opposed to those middle-class values that they were so anxious to flout were too dimly conceived to be used as a basis for any positive scheme.

These poets thus rejected the contemporary world without any clear understanding of why they rejected it, and without any clearly conceived substitute to offer. The positive values underlying Victorian life were beginning to crumble, and crumbling values are of no use to a poet. The place of the poet in society was ill defined not so much because the middle-class mind disliked poetry as because the traditional view of the poet's function was ceasing to be realizable, and there was not stability enough in value-patterns for a new one to emerge naturally or for the old one to become possible again. The only thing that remained stable was the poet's own emotions and sensations. On these, then, the poet took his stand, seeking when he could a religious tradition which would give some pattern to the exploitation of his emotions and sensations. But what the poet was really after was freedom for his sensibility, not a religious belief. He was willing to embrace that belief if it gave him that kind of freedom, whatever restrictions in other fields that might imply. The more conventional religious tradition was too much associated with the view of the poet as purveyor of uplift to be attractive. The other alternative was to play the part of licensed clown, and this, though undignified, at least meant freedom. It looked as though the poet would have to choose between clown and obscurantist. There is something of both in the poetry of the late nineteenth century, as the work of Wilde clearly shows.

Arthur Symons, Ernest Dowson, Lionel Johnson, and the other poets who belonged to the Rhymers' Club were concerned with winning greater freedom for sensibility than the conventional poetic tradition by then allowed. The influence exercised on them by the late romantic poets of France—by Verlaine and Rimbaud and Mallarmé, by the older Baudelaire—is understandable at once when we recognize that the French poets were seeking the same end. Though in attitude these English poets rejected the Tennysonian tradition, in technique they often simply extended it and refined on Tennyson's practices. Symbolism as a technique was not foreign to Tennyson's art and was present in some degree in all the poets of the English romantic tradition. Of course, symbolism of some kind is inherent in all art, but even the specific doctrines of the French Symbolists, the deliberate exploitation of sensation and its emotional accompaniments and associations within an extremely limited context, can be found illustrated in the work of Keats and Shelley and Tennyson. The poets of the Rhymers' Club, like the French Symbolists, differed from these, however, in regarding this technique as an end rather than as a means. Sensation and its accompanying emotions were not subordinated to a theme, but expressed because it was good to express them. The expression was a gesture of freedom, of individuality, a basing of art on the only value which for these poets had not been besmirched or annihilated by contemporary civilization —personal sensibility, and sensibility not to events but to sensations and to emotions derived from them. Thus it was not "art for art's sake" that they wanted at all (a meaningless phrase, anyway, because it implies no definition of art) but art for the sake of individual emotion, an emotion deriving not from events occurring in the outside world but from their own contemplation of objects chosen in advance for their ability to arouse the desired state of feeling.

These poets, then, unlike Tennyson and Browning and the poets of the Tennysonian tradition, turned their work into gestures of rejection of their age. But they still used the traditional medium. They used it with a difference, refining on certain aspects of it and eliminating others. By the end of the century this traditional medium was pretty much worn out. The type of poetic virtuosity represented by Tennyson had produced all it could, and already there were those who were experimenting in quite new techniques. Why the poets of the nineties did not feel themselves impelled to develop a new poetic medium as they developed a new attitude is not a difficult question to answer. They were seeking to retreat from a world they despised to a realm where they would be safe from the impingement of that world and its market-place values. They were willing enough to raise controversies about attitude and to shock the bourgeois mind, but they wanted their own realm to be safe, they wanted to be able to express those sensations and emotions of theirs with confidence and certainty. Their verse, for all its occasional sublety, is never really difficult. They did not wish to raise fundamental questions about the nature of the poetic medium. Though they played down the communicative aspect and played up the "self-expression" aspect of poetry, they did use a verse which was communicative, and in the traditional way. To have set about building up a whole new different poetic medium would have meant denying themselves the one certain thing they had. For all that has been said to the contrary, they did not really love language for itself but for its ability to express what they felt. And they had no great new message to give, which demanded a new medium of expression. They simply wanted to sit in a corner and express themselves, and, if that shocked the public, so much the better. In short, their attitude was too negative to demand a new medium. Had they opposed Victorian values with firmly held countervalues, or had they taken refuge simply in language, they might have achieved a technical revolution. But in the last resort they were simply traditional poets who wanted to be alone—alone with their sensations and emotions. The differentiating qualities of their work arise from this solitude, not from any revolutionary attitude.

Yet their attitude was different from that of their predecessors—they rejected contemporary life. Rejection, however, is a negative gesture only. Thus in attitude they mark the beginning of an important change (from acceptance to rejection) while as regards technique they simply played the final, rather tenuous, variations on an air which Keats had played and which Keats himself thought he had heard in Shakespeare.

CHAPTER II

THOMAS HARDY—A. E. HOUSMAN— GERARD MANLEY HOPKINS

THE 1890's saw a shift in the poet's conception of his own function from that of a public figure to a private one. If Tennyson had been asked what he conceived his duty to the public to be, he would have had a ready, and a positive, answer. But to the poets of the Rhymers' Club the question would hardly have made sense; they would have shaken their heads and replied that the poet had no such duty, that his only duty was to "art," which meant, of course, that his only duty was to himself. To put the matter crudely, the poet of the Tennysonian tradition was engaged in comforting the world, while the poet of the nineties (though employing what was in essence the Tennysonian technique) rejected the world because it could not comfort him, and engaged in comforting himself. This is true, at least, of one group of poets—the so-called "decadents"—of the period. There were others, some of whom continued the Tennysonian tradition, some adapting it to changed conditions, and others again who rejected it in quite a different way.

The pessimism of Thomas Hardy, as expressed both in his poetry and in his novels, can be contrasted with the prevailing attitude of the orthodox Victorians. The origins of Hardy's pessimism are well concealed. A writer who appears to bear a grudge against the

17

universe may not be aware himself of the reason why he bears that grudge. Hardy's own diagnosis of his pessimism wavered. Sometimes he objected to the blind chance that ruled the world:

> . . . . How arrives it joy lies slain
> And why unblooms the best hope ever sown?
> —Crass Casualty obstructs the sun and rain,
> And dicing Time for gladness casts a moan. . . . .
> These purblind Doomsters had as readily strown
> Blisses about my pilgrimage as pain.

But if all depends on mere chance, there is at least a fifty-fifty chance of happiness, which Hardy denies. Sometimes he professes to believe that it is not blind chance but a malignant fate that has control. Sometimes, again, the gods are pictured as simply ironical. The explanation varies, but the pessimism—for all the occasional glimpses of happiness, as in "Lyonesse" and "The Market Girl"—remains. At bottom, it appears to be based on an uneasiness concerning the whole Victorian scheme of life and society; hints and savage suggestions to this effect flicker throughout the poems and the novels, yet the point is never openly stated. In his unwieldy dramatic poem *The Dynasts* he attempts to deal with the matter through a mythologizing of the forces of history, yet the conclusion is doubtful and the mythological figures ambiguous. Hardy swam beyond the sunny Victorian shore where Browning romped and Tennyson paddled, and his feet lost the bottom. Yet why he swam out and where he was going he was unable to say.

For Hardy, the Victorian value scheme cracked up sooner than for most. Yet, because his disillusionment anticipated the more general breakdown of those values, he was less able than later writers to account for it or to rationalize it. He was never sure of his function as an artist, one way or the other. Technically, he was careless, indifferent: he grabbed whatever forms were to hand and used them as he needed them. His poetry has rhythm and rhyme, and that is about all that can be said. There is a ruggedness in his verse as there is a looseness in the plot structure of his novels, and neither was the result of the application of any theories about form or style. He gathered up all the data he could find that encouraged his pessimism and threw them magnificently and carelessly at the face of Heaven and his public. He heard the Victorian foundations creaking and mistook the sound for the ironic laughter of the gods.

The pessimism of A. E. Housman presents a similar problem. Its origin is not clear in his poetry, but we are given occasional hints in his prose work—in his lecture on poetry and in his scholarly essays on classical texts. "How the world is managed, and why it was created, I cannot tell; but it is no feather-bed for the repose of sluggards," he informs us in the midst of a discussion of textual criticism. This is precisely where he differed from the poet of the Tennysonian tradition, who *did* profess to know why the world was created and how it was managed, or at least felt it his duty to try to find out. (Tennyson spent a lot of time on that job.) Like Hardy, Housman is unhappy, pessimistic, and the reason, though perhaps neither knew it, is that each saw the Victorian base crumbling or as having crumbled. Housman projects his pessimistic emo-

tion into the melodramatic figure of the Shropshire
lad, who passes from inexperience to sorrow, from illusion to bitter disillusion, from content to regret:

> That is the land of lost content,
>   I see it shining plain,
> The happy highways where I went
>   And cannot come again.

There is nothing to do but bear it out stoically and
wait for death—which, if it comes by hanging, or
shooting in battle, is all the more grimly appropriate.

Housman's plea for the functionlessness of art and of
scholarship (for that is what his lecture on poetry and
many of his scholarly papers amount to) is the cry of
a man for whom civilization has lost its value-patterns.
The echoing plangency of *A Shropshire Lad* and *Last
Poems* comes from the heart of a man who can find
nothing in the life and thought of his time that can,
on a long view, give life a meaning:

> Oh never fear man, nought's to dread,
>   Look not left nor right:
> In all the endless road you tread
>   There's nothing but the night.

And the day is no happier a symbol than the night:

> Yonder see the morning blink:
> The sun is up, and up must I,
> To wash and dress and eat and drink
> And look at things and talk and think
> And work, and God knows why.

Housman denied himself so much—turning from
Propertius, the Latin poet whose work he loved, to
devote his life's energies to editing instead the trivial
Manilius, repressing his enthusiasms, shrinking from

the light—because he could find no valid reason why
what he liked was worth doing, because he could find
no real basis on which to ground his life and work;
and, being sensitive, afraid to do what he could not
justify, he took the stoic view and saw himself living
to endure rather than to enjoy. Edmund Wilson explains Housman's "almost insane attempt to conceal
[his] blazing light under a bushel" as an "exaggeration
of the Englishman's code of understatement in connection with his achievements and conquests";[1] but
there is more to it than that. Honest idealist as he was
(though how he would have hated being called that!)
he was reluctant to engage in any activity whose value
could not be attested in his own eyes by some valid
standard. He could find no such standard. The only
real belief he held was that in his own integrity: his
basic emotion was pride. All other values had dis-
solved save this, the last. It is no coincidence that
James Joyce, as much unlike Housman in his life and
work as one artist could be unlike another, also threw
overboard all values except the pride and integrity of
the artist. Both writers were idealists without ideals,
which meant that their only ideal was integrity. And
in both cases it was the receding tide of traditional values that left them in that plight.

A receding tradition leaves many interesting phenomena in its wake, and the literary shore in the last
years of the nineteenth century and the early years of
the twentieth is strewn with a great variety of pebbles.
The aesthetes were opposed by poets who, though no
longer at ease in Zion in the large way that Tennyson

1 *The Triple Thinkers* (New York, 1938), pp. 97–98.

had been, tried aggressively to shown that poetry did have a positive function in contemporary civilization. But they were distinctly on the defensive—their aggressiveness shows that. Further, they had to limit their view of contemporary civilization to some particular phase; they could not but be aware, however dimly, of the disintegration, and their solution was to cultivate one little plot which might remain whole in the breakup of larger unities, and consider that plot as the world. The imperialistic toughness of Rudyard Kipling and his well-dressed shadow, Sir Henry Newbolt, shows a limitation both in subject matter and in attitude which is in immediate contrast with the large scope of the mid-Victorian poets. The courageous shouts of W. E. Henley, the chastened romanticism of Robert Louis Stevenson, the technical skill and light-hearted grace of Austin Dobson, the scholarly artificiality of Andrew Lang, the misty sentimentality of "Fiona Macleod" (William Sharp)—all these show the poet cultivating a very small garden, which he does not trouble to integrate with the landscape as a whole. And the so-called Georgian poets of the succeeding generation share this quality sometimes to an even greater degree, each choosing a favorite emotion and a favorite scene, and ringing a few select changes.

Robert Bridges, who lived from 1844 to 1930, thus completely spanning the Victorian and the modern periods, presents the picture of a scholarly and cultured poet whose work combines ethical interests with a connoisseur's mild experimentation in language. His technical experiments are not of great importance—their net result is to substitute a thin and languid speculative

murmur for the more orthodox metrics, with some sim-
plifications in spelling and punctuation. But his work
is interesting as showing the graceful petering-out of
an important tradition in English poetry—the Neo-
Platonic tradition, whose chief representatives are
Spenser and Shelley, interpreted with the "high serious" preoccupations of Matthew Arnold and a thin
lyrical grace which recalls the Elizabethan lyric only
to the extent that mulled wine recalls a vintage claret.
He possessed skill, scholarship, and a calm philosophic
eye for nature and the more placid aspects of the
human scene. His spirit is essentially Victorian, and
the Muse of English Poetry may be comforted by the
fact that the Victorian spirit made its final exit as a
scholar and a gentleman.

The Georgian poets, sitting in their quiet gardens in
the twilight of Europe, deserve a chapter to themselves;
they have often been too lightly dismissed, too easily
misjudged, and some clarification of their position and
their contribution is necessary.

Movements in literature, as in culture generally, do
not follow the strict chronology that the historian
would prefer, and poetry did not wait for the Victorian
tradition to wear out before beginning to build up a
new one. And therefore, before we proceed to a discussion of the Georgians, something must be said of
the rebel movements started well within the Victorian
period. We have already mentioned the changes in attitude manifested by the poets of the nineties. But the
Victorian tradition embraced more than a poetic attitude; it included also a view of the nature of the poetic
medium, and this was never fundamentally challenged

by the aesthetes. Tennyson might have regarded the work of the more extreme of the French Symbolists as extravagant, but he would have understood what they were doing and appreciated the view of language which underlay their poetic practice. But the practice of Gerard Manley Hopkins was something quite different; it represented a view of language and its function in poetry with which Tennyson could have had no sympathy at all. Hopkins was impelled toward this view less by an awareness of the disintegration of traditional conventions than by a stern personal problem for a complete understanding of which the psychologist rather than the sociologist must be called in. But the interesting fact is that, in solving a personal problem for himself, he pointed the way to a solution of a more general problem for poets who came some half a century later. This is a phenomenon which frequently confronts the historian of literature—a movement is started by causes which have little if anything to do with the requirements of what we might call the "cultural situation" at the time, but later a state of affairs arises where that movement suggests a solution to a problem which this time does arise from the cultural situation, and so it is taken up and developed. The nineteenth-century Jesuit looked at life very differently from the young left-wing poet of the 1930's, yet as regards poetic technique the former had a very strong influence on the latter. If we can understand this, we can understand not only a particular incident in literary history but also the way in which progress in the intellectual arts very often comes about. This is worth emphasizing, because the explanation of

the literature of a period with reference to the cultural
and the sociological background has so often been falsi-
fied by too slick and mechanical a view of the nature
of influence and causation.

In a letter to Robert Bridges, Hopkins once said: "I
cannot think of altering anything. Why should I? I do
not write for the public."[2] It is clear from this and
from much other evidence that Hopkins did not conceive himself, as poet, to have any public function. In
this he was directly opposed to the Tennysonian conception, which was in essence that of the poet as
prophet. Hopkins in his capacity as poet had no prophetic mission. Yet, on the other hand, he did not
write his poetry merely for the sake of "self-expression" as some later poets professed to do. The tremendous care and patience he expended on his art,
the rigor and discipline which marks all his poetic activity, his painstaking study of meter and prosody, and
the care he took in expounding his precise meaning
and intention to his few interested friends are all clear
indications that he laid great stress on the communicative aspect of his verse. Yet he shunned publication,
refused even to recognize the existence of the general
reading public, and had no contact with the contemporary world of letters besides his friendship with
Bridges, Coventry Patmore, and R. W. Dixon. The
fact that he became a Catholic and a Jesuit early in
his career explains something of his reticence and his
isolation, but it does not adequately explain his view
of the function of poetry and does not explain at all

[2] *The Letters of Gerard Manley Hopkins to Robert Bridges*, ed. C. C. Abbott
(London, 1935), p. 46.

the nature and origin of his earnest experiments with the poetic medium. There was something peculiarly personal and possessive about Hopkins' attitude to his poetry; his zealous labor, his uncompromising experimentation, seem to have sprung from a fierce pride in the mastery of words, in wresting language to fit experience, from a sense of power and control. Tennyson regarded language as a friendly medium, to be handled poetically in accordance with certain accepted conventions and with certain expectations on the part of his audience: language was to be considered before experience, and if the experience to be communicated "suffered a sea-change" in the process of poetic expression, that did not much matter. Poetry came before the world, and by "poetry" Tennyson meant language given rhythm and pattern in such a way as to please those to whom such rhythm and pattern had come to be associated with the expression of welcome truths in a satisfying manner. But to Hopkins the experience was all important, and language was no friend to be granted favors, but an enemy to be fought with until it had been molded to express the experience. The reality of the experience could only be adequately conveyed by the essential movement and pattern of the words, by the most scrupulously skilful disposition of language that would give the poem what he called "inscape," that inner unity and design which corresponds to the uniqueness, the actuality, of the experience expressed. He wrote to Bridges:

No doubt my poetry errs on the side of oddness . . . . but as air, melody, is what strikes me most of all in music and design in painting, so design, pattern or what I am in the habit of calling "inscape" is what I above all aim at in poetry. Now it is the virtue of design, pattern or inscape to be distinctive and it is the vice of distinctiveness to become queer. This vice I cannot have escaped.[3]

The design he speaks of is not of importance just *qua* design; its importance lies in its being that particular design which is the truth he wished to communicate. For Keats, truth was beauty and beauty truth, and for Tennyson experience was important in so far as it was capable of "poetic" expression; but for Hopkins a poem was worth while only if by its individuality it adequately represented some unique reality. A poem constructed with all the skill and beauty in the world was yet defective if it lacked that specific "inscape" which was more than merely a formal requirement, for it was the guaranty of truth. Poetry defective in this way was written in what Hopkins called "Parnassian." His theory of "Parnassian" was developed quite early, and it throws an interesting light on Hopkins' whole view of poetry. It is the dialect of great poets when they lacked the ultimate and authentic inspiration. It is what the poet as public figure would be bound to write to a large extent, and Hopkins found it to be the style of much of Tennyson.[4]

Hopkins' view of the nature of the poetic medium was thus bound up with his general view of the function

---

[3] *Ibid.*, p. 66. Cf. his letter to Coventry Patmore, where he finds fault with Yeats's youthful poem "Mosada" on the grounds that "the essential and only lasting thing [was] left out—what I call *inscape*, that is species or individually-distinctive beauty of style" (*Further Letters of Gerard Manley Hopkins*, ed. C. C. Abbott [London, 1938]).

[4] See his very interesting letter to A. W. M. Baillie, September 10, 1864, where he explains his view of "Parnassian" at length (*Further Letters*, pp. 69–72). Cf. *The Note-Books and Papers of G. M. Hopkins*, ed. Humphrey House (London, 1937), pp. 29–30.

of poetry. Poetry for him represented an attempt to wring from words an authenticity not to be found in the language of ordinary discourse or of other kinds of literature. His experimentation in meter and language arose from this attempt. But the basis of it all was a certain fierce honesty in facing experience. There was for him no poetic subject matter: any subject would do if only, as he put it in a letter to Bridges, you were "in earnest" with it. It was this honesty of his that sent him to the Catholic church and, once in that church, to the Jesuits. If he accepted Christianity, he must accept it fully and logically and give himself up to it entirely. But having taken this step there developed the problem of relating his perception of the external world—which was exceptionally vivid and acute —to his duty as a Jesuit. Gifted with a most subtle awareness both of things and of people, and glorying as he did in the exercise of that awareness (as his notebooks show), he had nevertheless the conviction that this vision must not be indued in for its own sake but placed at the service of his religion. A complicated problem for his own personality ensued. His observation of the natural world had to be fitted in with his religious mission, and the nature of the resultant experience was what he tried to express in verse. He took no facile way out. Though he agreed in a general way with those who maintained that all nature was a manifestation of the glory of God, he was not therefore content to write placid nature poems and let the religious thought be implicit. He tried to convey the complexity of his experience into his verse, and it is this that gives his poetry that strange, dynamic quality, that sense of straining against the current, which is found in no other contemporary poet. Indeed, his whole theory of "sprung rhythm" and counterpoint might be traced to this desire to express adequately a complex and even contradictory set of experiences. He looked at nature from a point of view at once humanist and theological; thus for every statement he made there was, as it were, an equal and opposite counterstatement. He had to establish communication on several levels at once, unlike his contemporaries, whose problems of experience were simpler. The self-questioning of Tennyson in *In Memoriam* was a simple and surface catechism, representing no fundamental duality of vision such as disturbed Hopkins. But Hopkins did have dual vision; he was at once man and priest, master and servant, lover of life and ascetic. If he had not been poetically gifted, the resulting problem would have been a personal, pyschological one, but being a poet the complexity of his experience forced him to a new view of the function of poetry and to daring experiments in poetic technique. From Dryden to Tennyson the English poets, living in a civilization whose intellectual basis was really a facile deism, had been faced by no problem of double vision. But Hopkins, going back to Rome with an anticipatory sense of the crumbling of this age-long compromise, was faced with a new complexity in experience. Yet it was not really new, for the metaphysical poets had faced and met the same problem. Like John Donne, Hopkins had to find a way of making poetic statements on several different levels at the same time.

The publication of Hopkins' poems by Bridges in

1918 and the subsequent influence he had on the younger poets of the late 1920's and early 1930's coincided with a great revival of interest in the metaphysical poets of the seventeenth century and the influence exerted by this revival on the modern poets. Both Hopkins and John Donne had reacted against the more popular modes of poetic expression in favor of a more difficult, a more personal, and a more urgent way of writing. If Donne tried to write on more levels than the Spenserian tradition allowed, so Hopkins attempted to write on more levels than were allowed by the Tennysonian tradition. Hopkins was not uniformly successful: the different levels of expression do not always integrate into a coherent and impressive whole, and this seems to have been due to a lack of integration in his own personality. Professor Abbott has an interesting remark to make in this connection:

They [certain of Hopkins' poems] are poems written to the glory of God by a man who is looking on the world as charged with His grandeur and revealing His bounty and presence. But always as I read them I feel that the poet is primarily seized by the beauty of earth, and that though a man of exquisitely tempered and religious mind, his senses, not his religion, are in the ascendant. . . . . The yeast of the religious spirit has not worked through them. The fusion of earthly beauty and exemplum is often so incomplete that the second is merely the addendum of a poet captive in the first place to the beauty beseiging his senses. . . . . There is something not altogether subdued to the Christian purpose in this side of the poet's work.[5]

But though certain defects in Hopkins' poetry may derive from unresolved conflicts in the poet's personality, it is equally true that the virtues derive from a very similar source, namely, the complexity and many-

[5] *The Letters of G. M. Hopkins to Robert Bridges*, pp. xxvii ff.

sidedness of his feeling. Both his obscurity and his brilliance arise out of this complexity, as the following example—the opening stanza of his poem on Henry Purcell—will show:

> Have fair fallen, O fair, fair have fallen, so dear
> To me, so arch-especial a spirit as heaves in Henry Purcell,
> An age is now since past, since parted; with the reversal
> Of the outward sentence low lays him, listed to a heresy,
> here.

The urgence of the adjective in the first line, the rapid movement of the verse which seems to want to keep the reader's reaction in suspense until it has completed the thought, the order of the words, the cadence of the phrases ("low lays him, listed to a heresy, here"), are all the marks of a poet whose attitude to his subject is compounded of many different and even conflicting visions all of which he must communicate at once if the truth is to be told. This will be made clear if we compare Hopkins' stanza with one from Tennyson:

> Now sleeps the crimson petal, now the white;
> Nor waves the cypress in the palace walk;
> Nor winks the gold fin in the porphyry font:
> The firefly wakens: waken thou with me.

Here diction, rhythm, and cadence contribute to a single and simple mood; there is no breathless haste to get the qualifying statements in before the reader can pause, no problem of fusion: there is but one level of statement, to which all undertones are carefully and placidly subordinated. Hopkins' verse, however, is not made up of dominant meaning to which undertones contribute; his meanings are all equal tones, which must be fused, not subordinated. An analysis of that difficult but fascinating poem "Tom's Garland" will show Hopkins wrestling with the same problem. All the devices which for the casual reader produce only obscurity are really intended to prevent the reader from understanding anything until he can understand everything. For the complete statement alone—elaborated, qualified, compressed, unified—is the truth. As he said in a letter to Bridges: "One of two kinds of obscurity one should have—either the meaning to be felt without effort as fast as one reads or else, if dark at first reading, when once made out to *explode*." This term "explode" is significant: it conveys the sense of everything happening at once, which is so important for Hopkins. What Hopkins seems to be saying in this sentence is that one should write either as Tennyson does, from a single point of view, with one mood, one meaning, one simple truth to tell, in which case that mood is set right away and the lines merely continue it without modifying or complicating it; or else in the many-visioned way that he employs himself, where the truth is kept in suspense until all is told, for to understand a line before completing the stanza would be to learn a half-truth or a falsehood.

Hopkins' view of "sprung rhythm" and his general metrical practice have been sufficiently discussed by the critics; our purpose here is not to expound them but to attempt to explain them. Hopkins was a poet with unusual problems of personal adjustment who was driven to seek a kind of integrity in his poetry that demanded a new technique and also a denial of the poet's public function. For what audience did he write? He probably could not have answered that question himself. Though he told Bridges that he wrote not for the public but for him, we are obviously meant to take this in a symbolic rather than a literal sense. There is no doubt that Hopkins did wish for some kind of readers, "fit audience though few," yet he is never explicit on the subject. He certainly had no desire to appeal to the great public who read and enjoyed Tennyson, though not for reasons of snobbery. This uncertainty about his audience he shares with many of the poets of our own generation, who, faced with the splitting-up of the poetry-reading public, cannot make up their minds for whom to write. This was a much wider problem in the world after 1919 than it was in Hopkins' time, for in the former period the widespread disintegration of older values and beliefs had taken the solid ground from underneath the poets and they were doubtful alike of their function and of their readers. Coterie poetry, poetry of personal allusion and symbol, which developed in the 1920's, was one answer to this problem. But this is a matter to be discussed in a later chapter; the point to be emphasized here is that, different as he was in so many important ways from the young English poets of the late 1920's and early 1930's, Hopkins shared many of their problems. His problems derived largely from personal factors, while theirs was the result of the general state of culture and even of civilization as a whole. Yet both he and they were faced with the problem of communicating on several levels at once, of determining anew not only who was to be their audience but what was the nature and function of their art, of building something to replace the Tennysonian tradition. That the metaphysical poets of the seventeenth century were also faced with this manifold problem, for yet different reasons, is in part the explanation of why John Donne and Gerard Manley Hopkins lie behind so much modern poetry.

In America, Walt Whitman's rebellion against the current poetic tradition represented in some ways an intention diametrically opposed to that of Hopkins. For while Hopkins was renouncing the Tennysonian conception of the poet as a public figure, it was the public aspect of the poet's function—the poet as prophet—that Whitman manifested to a unique degree. Yet they had in common an impatience with the traditional poetic treatment of language which makes their techniques in some ways comparable. Both leaped at the throat of language in their endeavor to wrest from it the meaning that mattered; but for Hopkins this meant a new and formidable metrical discipline, while for Whitman it meant simply complete freedom. Whitman, the democratic individualist, was trying to extend the scope of poetry to enable it to express and reflect with complete immediacy and without undue formality all the surging moods of man conceived at the same time as individual and as integral part of the democratic mass: Hopkins, the austere Jesuit yet clear-eyed lover of the external world, was trying to evolve a new poetic discipline which would enable him to express the complex awareness which his twofold attitude brought him. Thus Hopkins is difficult because he has to communicate his thought on several levels at once, while Whitman is breathless and sometimes almost incoherent because he has to communicate, though on a single level, many thoughts at the same time. Both shared a fundamental honesty; they would compromise neither with life nor with language, and both regarded language not as a master to be worshiped but as a recalictrant servant to be coerced. "I always knew in my heart," wrote Hopkins to Bridges in 1882, "Walt Whitman's mind to be more like my own than any other man's living. As he is a very great scoundrel this is not a pleasant confession. And this also makes me the more desirous to read him and the more determined that I will not."[6] Their ideals were opposed, but their methods of trying to realize them were not dissimilar.

Whitman had two kinds of influence on the English poets, as prophet and as poetic technician. His influence as propet was felt first, most clearly in the work of Edward Carpenter, who lived long enough (1844–1929) to combine the teaching of Whitman with that of D. H. Lawrence into rather loose prophecy. More recent English poets, such as W. H. Auden and Cecil Day Lewis, have been influenced less by Whitman's ideas (though they seem to have learned more here than is generally admitted) than by the movement of his verse, which is traceable in much of their work. The influence of Whitman's thought on modern English writers is nearly always seen interpreted through ideas of D. H. Lawrence, partly because Carpenter, the first to make this fusion, is often the middleman through whom Whitman reaches them.

The English poets who came to maturity after the the great war were faced with many problems. The audience for poetry was neither as distinct nor as homo-

6 *Ibid.*, p. 155.

geneous as it had been in Tennyson's generation; both the function of poetry and the poet's place in society were in doubt; the sources of imagery which had been traditional for English poetry for generations had for a variety of reasons become dried up. All this had the result, first, of making English poetry more "metaphysical," more ambivalent in expression, more complicated in attitude; second, of sending the poets in search of new and more violent sources of imagery, which in turn encouraged a change of attitude toward the poetic medium in general; and, third, of making them either completely private figures, addressing personal friends and fellow-members of the coterie with the help of private symbols, or, in their resentment against a disintegrating social background which was depriving them of any assured status, public figures of revolt and revolution (as opposed to the orthodox prophetic role of Tennyson, representing the poet as public figure in a very different sense). The nature of the situation is perhaps most clearly indicated when we see—as we do in the early work of Auden—a poet conducting a public mission through purely private images and symbols.

Thus the nineteenth century flowed into the twentieth in many different ways. There was the overflow of the Tennysonian tradition, which is still with us, though continually decreasing in importance. There was the aesthetic and the Symbolist tradition, which, while fundamentally Tennysonian in its attitude to the poetic medium, was the reverse in its view of the poet's function. There was aggressive traditionalism manifesting itself in such ways as the imperialism of Kipling but showing by its very aggressiveness that it was on the defensive. There was the Catholic devotional tradition (in which, in spite of his devotional poetry, it would be wrong to place Hopkins) remaining outside of the current, cloistered from the world. There were the pastoral and regional traditions, little streams now, though they had been wide and deep in the seventeenth century, that trickled into the gardens of the Georgian poets—poets who sunned themselves gently in the green Indian Summer of Old England, a little sad but not sorry. And then, as the century proceeds and changes in the modern world become more apparent, Hopkins becomes influential, Whitman is read, and John Donne and the other metaphysical poets become the recognized masters. How twentieth-century poetry developed as the result of these traditions and these influences is the subject of the succeeding chapters.

CHAPTER III

GEORGIAN POETRY

AT THE end of 1912 there appeared an anthology of recent poetry entitled *Georgian Poetry, 1911–12*, edited by Edward Marsh. It was the first of five such volumes which appeared every second year until 1922. Marsh introduced the first volume with a statement of its function:

> This volume is issued in the belief that English poetry is now once again putting on a new strength and beauty.
>
> Few readers have the leisure or the zeal to investigate each volume as it appears; and the process of recognition is often slow. This collection, drawn entirely from the publications of the last two years, may if it is fortunate help the lovers of poetry to realize that we are at the beginning of another "Georgian period" which may take rank in due time with the several great poetic ages of the past.

Here, at the very beginning of the reign of George V, was a group of poets who consciously proclaimed themselves as "Georgians," giving a name to their period when it had scarcely begun, and self-conscious about their place in history to an extent unparalleled among artists who were not revolutionaries or innovators on a grand scale. Yet these poets had nothing very new to say; neither their subject matter nor their technique was in any degree original. They took traditional pastoral motives, romantic accounts of the East, nature subjects, meditative descriptions of English scenery, or accounts in a subdued lyrical strain of personal experiences in listening to birds or watching sunsets, and produced what was on the whole a quiet, unambitious verse, restrained in mood and low in temperature. The prevailing form was a somewhat undisciplined blank verse, though lyrical stanzas of various kinds were also common. It was a simple poetry, easy to understand, written on a single level, posing no problems and solving none. Why, then, the pretentious introduction, the fanfare of trumpets hailing a new era?

To find the answer to this question we must inquire further. Why, we might ask, did these poets find it desirable to seek communal publication in anthologies? Anthology publication of contemporary verse is rare in English literature. We find it in the sixteenth century in *Tottel's Miscellany* and similar publications modeled on it. We find an example of it at the beginning of the Irish revival in *Poems and Ballads of Young Ireland* (1888). Each of these anthologies was something in the nature of a manifesto. The poets who contributed were experimenters or conscious participators in a new movement, and the collection they compiled was partly an advertisement, showing the public what the "new school" could do, partly a statement of policy, making manifest their aims by example, partly a challenge, hurled in the face of traditionalists who did not accept their way of writing. Similar in purpose, though less representative of a whole group, was the *Lyrical Ballads* of 1798 where Wordsworth and Coleridge combined to enunciate and illustrate a new view of poetry. The Georgian anthologies were obviously not of this nature; neither their aims nor their methods were particularly new. True, the contributors believed that they were at the beginning of a great new poetic period, but they did not explain in virtue of what contribution of theirs it was to be great. Edward Marsh's introductory note was anything but a manifesto. Poetry was "putting on a new strength and beauty," he wrote, but strength and beauty were not qualities contributed to poetry by the Georgians; they were qualities of all good earlier poetry, and the sense in which they were to become "new" as from 1911 was left vague.

Yet these poets must have banded together for some purpose. There are two main reasons which compel men to combine into armies—attack and defense. If, unlike the contributors to the other anthologies cited, the Georgian poets were not making an attack, the possibility suggests itself that their common purpose was one of defense. And this seems to be the truth of the matter. If we scan the body of poetry published in these volumes and endeavor to see its place in the development of post-Victorian literature, it is not difficult to realize that the common aim of the Georgian poets was retrenchment. In response to the crumbling of older conventions and attitudes they adopted an eclectic traditionalism, limited, refined, carefully hedged round, and within these confines sang softly but confidently. They were not in any real sense "escapists." They chose for theme and background those aspects of England which were still amenable to treatment in the traditional way. They tended to become "regional" poets, each celebrating the acres of the countryside he knew and loved best. The sea, the country town, and selected rural parts of England made up the bulk of their subject matter. Some, in the traditional romantic way, turned to the East for glamour and mystery, but such attempts were rarely successful, resulting in vague and florid rhetoric. Georgian poetry was at its best when it responded, quietly meditative, to the slow-beating rustic heart of England. It was not an original or a profound poetry; the subject was pretty threadbare by now, and a tendency to repetition and embroidery was difficult to avoid. Yet, in its own thin way, it was genuine. The search for certainty in a disrupting world, combined with the conviction that certainty must be salvaged from the past rather than born again in the future, gave these writers a certain tremulous stability. Their common attitude is best symbolized by the concluding lines of Rupert Brooke's "The Old Vicarage, Grantchester," which appeared in the first volume of the series:

> Say, do the elm-clumps greatly stand,
> Still guardians of that holy land?
> The chestnuts shade, in reverend dream,
> The yet unacademic stream?
> Is dawn a secret shy and cold
> Anadyomene, silver-gold?
> And sunset still a golden sea
> From Haslingfield to Madingley?
> And after, ere the night is born,
> Do hares come out about the corn?
> Oh, is the water sweet and cool,
> Gentle and brown, above the pool?
> And laughs the immortal river still
> Under the mill, under the mill?
> Say, is there Beauty yet to find?
> And Certainty? and Quiet kind?
> Deep meadows yet, for to forget
> The lies, and truths, and pain? . . . . oh! yet
> Stands the Church clock at ten to three?
> And is there honey still for tea?

These lines might well stand as the motto of the Georgian poets. They sought "Beauty," "Certainty," and "Quiet kind" in those aspects of their civilization which showed no signs of change, which had not yet responded to the crumbling of traditions that had already affected other aspects of art and thought. But so far the sleepy hollows of England had not yet developed into a waste land—at least not for these poets.

The question asked by these lines of Rupert Brooke's is really, "stands England where she did?" And in order that it might be answered in the affirmative, England has to be defined in a very narrow sense. Georgian poetry on the whole tends to be regional and patriotic, and both the regionalism and the patriotism are part of the quest for certainty. There is rustic England and, for contrast, the mysterious East. Thus W. J. Turner expressed his love for the former:

> I love the mossy quietness
> That grows upon the great stone flags,
> The dark tree-ferns, the staghorn ferns,
> The pre-historic antlered stags
> That carven stand and stare among
> The silent, ferny wilderness.

And, in the same volume, he pays his tribute to the latter:

> When I was but thirteen or so
> I went into a golden land,
> Chimborazo, Cotopaxi
> Took me by the hand.

Or again:

> Beyond the blue, the purple seas,
> Beyond the thin horizon's line,
> Beyond Antilla, Hebrides,
> Jamaica, Cuba, Caribbees,
> There lies the land of Yucatan.

This is a simple romantic emotion, deriving as much from a naïve love of melodious and strange names as from any interest in adventure. We find just the same sort of contrast in Walter De la Mare:

> When thin-strewn memory I look through,
> I see most clearly poor Miss Loo,
> Her tabby cat, her cage of birds,
> Her nose, her hair—her muffled words,
> And how she'd open her green eyes,
> As if in some immense surprise,
> Whenever, as we sat at tea,
> She made some small remark to me.

This is England. And then there is the East:

> Far are the shades of Arabia
>   Where the princes ride at noon,
> 'Mid the verdurous vales and thickets,
>   Under the ghost of the moon;
> And so dark is that vaulted purple
>   Flowers in the forest rise
> And toss into blossom 'gainst the phantom stars
>   Pale in the noonday skies.

De la Mare is best known, perhaps, for his treatment of fairy themes and moods of quiet mystery. The familiar and the mysterious being the two dominant notes of Georgian poetry, De la Mare tries to bring them close together by domiciling mystery in rural England instead of always seeking it in remote countries.

The inclosed preserves of the Georgian poets were very like each other. Though each had his own favorite spot in which to lay out his garden, so that between them they covered most of England, the pictures they have to show us have a strong family resemblance. Here is Wilfrid Wilson Gibson's moorland:

> The sky was cloudless overhead,
> And just alive with larks asinging;

And in a twinkling I was swinging
Across the windy hills, lighthearted.
A kestrel at my footstep started,
Just pouncing on a frightened mouse,
And hung o'erhead with wings a-hover . . . .

Here is the rural scene as given by Francis Ledwidge:

And sweet the little breeze of melody
The blackbird puffs upon the budding tree,
While the wild poppy lights upon the lea
And blazes 'mid the corn.

The skylark soars the freshening shower to hail,
And the meek daisy holds aloft her pail,
And Spring all radiant by the wayside pale
Sets up her rock and reel.

Here is John Drinkwater on Sussex:

For peace, than knowledge more desirable,
Into your Sussex quietness I came,
When summer's green and gold and azure fell
Over the world in flame.

And peace upon your pasture-lands I found,
Where grazing flocks drift on continually,
As little clouds that travel with no sound
Across a windless sky.

Out of your oaks the birds call to their mates
That brood among the pines, where hidden deep
From curious eyes a world's adventure waits
In columned choirs of sleep.

John Freeman discovers beauty in the countryside:

Beauty walked over the hills and made them bright.
She in the long fresh grass scattered her rains
Sparkling and glittering like a host of stars,
But not like stars cold, severe, terrible.
Hers was the laughter of the wind that leaped
Arm-full of shadows, flinging them far and wide.
Hers the bright light within the quickening green
Of every new leaf on the oldest tree.

Here Harold Monro has left London for the country:

> The fresh air moves like water round a boat.
> The white clouds wander. Let us wander too.
> The whining, wavering plover flap and float.
> That crow is flying after that cuckoo.
> Look! Look! . . . . They're gone. What are the
>   great trees calling?
> Just come a little farther, by that edge
> Of green, to where the stormy ploughland, falling
> Wave upon wave, is lapping to the hedge.

Edmund Blunden describes perch-fishing:

> On the far hill the cloud of thunder grew
> And sunlight blurred below; but sultry blue
> Burned yet on the valley water where it hoards
> Behind the miller's elmen floodgate boards,
> And there the wasps, that lodge them ill-concealed
> In the vole's empty house, still drove afield
> To plunder touchwood from old crippled trees
> And build their young ones their hutched nurseries;
> Still creaked the grasshoppers' rasping unison
> Nor had the whisper through the tansies run
> Nor weather-wisest bird gone home.

W. H. Davies was the most faithful of all to his country plot:

> Yes, I will spend the livelong day
> With Nature in this month of May;
> And sit beneath the trees, and share
> My bread with birds whose homes are there;
> While cows lie down to eat, and sheep
> Stand to their necks in grass so deep;
> While birds do sing with all their might,
> As though they felt the earth in flight.

Gordon Bottomley frequently turned from his poetic dramas to join in the rustic chorus, though his note is more individual:

> The long town ends at Littleholme, where the road
> Creeps up to hills of ancient-looking stone.

Under the hanging eaves at Littleholme
A latticed casement peeps above still gardens
Into a crown of druid-solemn trees
Upon a knoll as high as a small house,
A shapely mound made so by nameless men
Whose smoothing touch yet shows through the green hide.

All these poems were published in the Georgian anthologies, and they show a common search for certainty in quiet places. The English countryside is consciously linked up with England's past. The poets seem to have their eyes averted from something: here, they seem to say, is a subject which we can contemplate with peace of mind, here we can find tradition, continuity, stability. It is not a fake pastoralism; the countryside is real, the emotion is genuine. Only occasionally, as in some of Sturge Moore's pastorals, do we find shepherds and shepherdesses with Greek names framed in a classical setting. Yet the evident desire to see the part as the whole—to see these dreamy rustic scenes as England—indicates a certain deliberate lack of perspective. It is as though these poets joined hands and published communally in anthologies because they were afraid. It was a vague fear of the disintegration of something they could not name, and against this Edward Marsh's anthologies were conceived as a defense.

But though this is the dominant note in the poetry of the Georgian anthologies, it is by no means the only one. Echoes of the Pre-Raphaelites and the aesthetic modes of the nineties are still to be found. There is also to be noted a vein of realistic urban observation which endeavors to present aspects of modern city life in a verse which is traditional in all respects except occasionally in its imagery. There are in addition poets whose contributions to these anthologies do not at all represent the scope of their work as a whole. Wilfrid Wilson Gibson, for example, who contributes some rustic incidents to these collections, was primarily a narrative poet whose main interest lay in depicting the lives of farmers in his native Northumberland and of workers in English industrial towns. After the thin romantic verse of his earliest publications, he produced in *Daily Bread* (1910) a series of poetic studies in dramatic form dealing, in a way which curiously mingles melodrama with careful realism, with moments of crisis in the lives of farmers, fisherfolk, and workers chiefly in Northumberland. Though full of traditional melodramatic properties—a strange woman staggering into a cottage to give birth to a dead child before dying herself with a word of forgiveness for her betrayer, and similar incidents—these poems have a somber vigor which is unlike anything produced at the period and is distinctly reminiscent of Crabbe. Gibson dropped the dramatic form in his later poems, and in *Fires* (1912), *Thoroughfares* (1914), and *Livelihood* (1917) gives, in impressive and unadorned verse, graphic accounts of aspects of working-class life. He was obviously more interested in his subject than in the treatment—the versification is sometimes quite crude—and his choice of the dramatic incident to illuminate the drab background gives his poetry real power and conviction. In *Borderlands* (1914) and occasionally in later poems he returned to the dramatic form of *Daily Bread*, but fundamentally all his poetry is dramatic in its intensity and its insistence on the single incident. He makes effective use of Northumberland dialect, which helps to emphasize the proletarian note. He had a real gift for illuminating the normal lives of the people he dealt with by etching vividly the moment of crisis or of passion, and he could command, too, the single image:

> Her day out from the workhouse-ward, she stands,
> A grey-haired woman, decent and precise,
> With prim black bonnet and neat paisley shawl,
> Among the other children by the stall,
> And with grave relish eats a penny ice.
>
> To wizened toothless gums with quaking hands
> She holds it, shuddering with delicious cold,
> Nor heeds the jeering laughter of young men . . . .

But the dramatic qualities of his best verse cannot be illustrated by brief quotation.

The Georgian anthologies took no cognizance of the kind of verse that Gibson spent most of his time writing and selected extracts that were not typical of his work, such as "The Hare," an uncharacteristic poem from *Fires*. Only a very few aspects of Gibson's work would have contributed to the Georgian retrenchment.

Another poet whose most characteristic work was not represented in the Georgian anthologies, though he did contribute to them, was John Masefield. Like Gibson, he was primarily a narrative poet, dealing both in the short narrative ballad and in the long tale. And, again like Gibson, he preferred to write of humble folk, expressing his aim with a certain grandiose self-consciousness in his poem "A Consecration":

> Not the ruler for me, but the ranker, the tramp of the road,
> The slave with the sack on his shoulders pricked on with
>   the goad,
> The man with too weighty a burden, too weary a load.

The sailor, the stoker of steamers, the man with the clout,
The chantyman bent at the halliards, putting a tune to
   the shout,
The drowsy man at the wheel and the tired lookout.

His ballads have a thin vigor of their own, and his
faculty for observation combined with his knowledge
of sea life helped an undistinguished style to achieve
conviction. His longer tales were written under Chaucerian inspiration—he himself tells us, in the Preface
to his collected poems (1918), that the *Parliament of
Fowls* converted him to poetry. In speed and slickness
of narrative *The Everlasting Mercy* (1911) does show
Chaucerian influence, but *The Widow in the Bye Street*
(1912), *Dauber* (1912), and *The Daffodil Fields* (1913)
have little suggestion of the early poet. The observation is close and clear, individual passages of description rise to considerable heights, but the stories as a
whole mean much less than the author thought they
did. Fundamentally a traditionalist and an idealist,
Masefield uses realism as an incidental technique, a
means to achieve a moral end whose function in the
story is never very clear. A process of evaporation goes
on, and though there are passages of strength and vigor
that strike us as we read them, by the time we reach
the end of the tale there seems to be nothing left.
Reynard the Fox (1919), a more straightforward and
highly colorful poem with distinct Chaucerian suggestions, is perhaps the most successful of all Masefield's
narrative pieces.

Both Gibson and Masefield are in a sense lost poets.
Gibson was primarily concerned with aspects of the
contemporary social scene, but the tradition which he

accepted from the earlier poets had little provision for the sort of thing he was interested in. You could adopt the Wordsworthian attitude to the peasant and imitate *Michael*, you could employ the harsh moral realism of Crabbe, you could use a Browningesque dramatic monologue, but none of these provided adequate forms for the matter which Gibson wished to express. He had not the energy or the originality to work out forms adequate to his subject matter, and he remains a transitional poet whose work is characterized by a struggle between form and content. He was implicated in the Georgian retrenchment to the extent that he conceived of both the function and the medium of poetry in the traditional way, yet in spite of this he seems to have been searching for a new attitude. This accounts for the feeling we often have while reading his poetry today—that he is a poet rather hesitantly pouring new wine into old bottles. Masefield faced a similar conflict. At heart a sentimentalist and a moralist of the old school, a believer in Beauty in the Tennysonian sense, he yet chose as his subject matter the "tough" aspects of contemporary life. The conflict however was less real in his case than in that of Gibson, for he was moved by no new social attitude. The ugly side of the social scene was for him picturesque because of its ugliness, and toughness was romantic. The meditative heartiness—strange combination!—that emerges from his work has a sort of dude-ranch quality. Later in his career Masefield gave up the struggle and cut the Gordian knot by reverting to a rather tedious traditionalism. Had he lived in an age when the cultural tradition was at once stable and vigorous, he might have done more justice to his talents.

The Georgian anthologies therefore represented only one of several strains of poetry in the period. Their poems indicate an attempt to keep alive, though in an attenuated form, a tradition which was at once Wordsworthian and Tennysonian, without the prophetic aspects of either of these poets. Meditation, nature, the rustic scene (and, for romantic relief, the Orient), England conceived as the past manifesting itself in the present, occasionally a devotional note, and behind everything an optimism, sometimes subdued, sometimes boisterous—this is what we see as we turn the leaves of *Georgian Poetry*. Occasionally we run across a poet whose work proclaims him to be not at home among his fellows. The poetry of D. H. Lawrence, with its intense individual mythmaking, is obviously out of place here. His verse has an un-Georgian vigor and originality, springing from a personal maladjustment whose origins are at once psychological and sociological. The expression here is not on a single and simple level; Lawrence's poems are not meditative observations nor are they fables designed to illustrate a point of view (and most Georgian poetry falls into one of these two classes); they are fables designed to test a hypothesis. The complexity of feeling, with resultant complexity of structure and imagery, which one finds in such a poem as "Snap-Dragon" is due to its being a poem of exploration, of discovery, where the imagery begins by being ambivalent and ends by dropping alternative meanings, the problem having been worked through, the hypothesis tested, the vision achieved. There is always something disturbing about such poetry, for the reader is watching the poet in a process of self-discovery, neither reader nor writer being aware of the end of the journey until it is attained. Lawrence's intensity and impatience led him to construct his poetry in such a way that the poem concludes at the point where most writers would begin—with the achievement of an interpretation of the phenomena which are being described. The poem becomes a myth in virtue of its conclusion, too late to let the previous imagery fall into line. Lawrence was not concerned in the Georgian retrenchment; in fact, his was the opposite problem: having abandoned all tradition as ceasing to have validity for him, he sought a purely personal interpretation of all phenomena, physical and psychological, human and natural. Less confident in his conclusions than Blake, whose aim was similar, he escaped the charge of madness because he never remained in one position long enough to elaborate an original symbolism for explaining it. And it is unfamiliar symbols that disturb the public more than unfamiliar truths.

Lawrence, therefore, was not on the Georgian side: he did not respond to the crumbling of traditional values and attitudes by an attempt at conservation. He belonged to the group which did not become dominant in poetry until some years later, the group whose interest lay in applying alternatives to the English poetic tradition which had come through the nineteenth century. But there was this difference: Lawrence was really concerned not with a poetic tradition at all but with a more general discovery of truth. He was included first among the Georgians and later among the

Imagists by pure accident, and he was really an enemy within both camps.

What the younger poets and critics have most noticed about the typical Georgians is the thinness of their poetry. There is no more in it than meets the eye. It is statement all on one level. This kind of simplicity had been a feature of English poetry for two centuries, and, as we have noted in discussing Hopkins, it was implied in the Tennysonian tradition. But in the Georgians this quality is found in an even higher degree. Not only, as in Pope or Wordsworth or Tennyson, is the imagery organized in order to emphasize the surface thought (instead of, as in Shakespeare or Donne, to set up both confirmations and countersuggestions, making the total poem both more complex and more inclusive) but the surface thought itself has no richness. Consider these lines from W. H. Davies:

> Thy beauty haunts me heart and soul,
>   Oh thou fair Moon, so close and bright;
> Thy beauty makes me like the child
>   That cries aloud to own thy light;
> The little child that lifts each arm
> To press thee to her bosom warm.

There is a peculiarly simple set of relationships here. The relation of the poet to the moon's beauty is identified with that of a child to the moon—not to the child's relationship to some quite different object. The introduction of the child in this stanza has no real meaning, no further point is made, no richness is added. The poet is inclosed in a tiny little world where everyone is looking at the moon and every relationship must be a relationship to the moon. There are several concepts here—beauty, the moon, the poet, the child. The poet is to the moon's beauty as the child is to the moon. The distinction between the moon and its beauty is deliberately blurred, as is that between the poet and the child. And as no simile can be effective without an awareness of dissimilarity (you only gain a point by comparing *A* to *B* if there is sufficient initial difference between *A* and *B* to make the comparison informative) the effect is repetitive rather than illuminating. Then consider the second (and final) stanza of this short poem:

> Though there are birds that sing this night
>   With thy white beams across their throats,
> Let my deep silence speak for me
>   More than for them their sweetest notes:
> Who worships thee till music fails
> Is greater than thy nightingales.

Here the birds are introduced—also in their relations to the moon. The child image is dropped completely; it is left hanging in the air and no further tieup is made. A simple contrast is made between the birds, who pay tribute to the moon by singing, and the poet, who also pays tribute to the moon, only by silence. The conclusion—that the latter mode of paying tribute is better than the former—is unprepared for in terms of the imagery and structure of the poem, and so the poem comes to rest on an arbitrary conclusion. In this little world where everyone is concerned only with the moon and loose identifications and differentiations are made between the fundamentally indistinguishable inhabitants there can be no possibility of richness of statement. If a great lyric is one which combines adequacy of pattern with richness of implication (and literature, as opposed to journalism, might be defined as pattern with maximum implication), such a lyric cannot be called great. But there are other, if minor, qualities in poetry which may result in value, if not in the highest value, and before Georgian poetry is dismissed it might be well to consider what qualities it does possess and what the resulting value of the poetry is.

The Georgians were careful and precise observers, but they kept their gaze turned away from anything that might remind them of change. Within the limits which they set themselves their quiet realism often produced simple poems of acquiescence in the natural world, which, without the inclusiveness of the best metaphysical poetry or the philosophic basis of Wordsworth, embodied patterns of static emotion which can still be communicated to the pleasure and refreshment of the reader. What the seventeenth-century poets did by multiple attitudes and ambivalent imagery, the nineteenth-century poets did by grounding their observation on philosophy: the Georgians had neither multiplicity nor philosophy, for neither was allowed them by the conditions of their time, and they tried to compensate by naïveté. In achieving their retrenchment they had to cut their losses, and their position would have been less secure had they attempted complexity of attitude or involved themselves in philosophies which were subject to attack and disintegration. The result was that they did attain some mastery over what might be called the static lyric, a kind of poetry where the movement is either nonexistent or repetitious, where all implications are confined within the single initial situation, and where attitude is adequate to the given situation *and no more*. With Wordsworth, an attitude to a tree or a peasant was, as the result of a wider definition implied nonetheless within the poem simply describing the tree, also an attitude to life, to the world. With Donne, the paradox of woman's love was expressed in such a way that it became also the paradox of divine love and more besides—the statement of a universal problem; and this not through explicit analogy but through complexity of imagery and structure. With the Georgians the attitude was just sufficient to cover the subject matter. You meditated in a treeful manner about a tree, and there was an omnilunar quality in what you said about the moon. Any enlargement of implication would have been dangerous; it would have threatened your carefully fenced-in preserve and let in the factors that made for change. As a result of these drastic limitations Georgian poetry, at its best, has at least the negative virtues of lacking bombast, excess of zeal, perhaps the vice to which poetry is most prone. Being unpretentious, it does not irritate by the gap between promise and achievement. The "vatic" function is dropped altogether, and the poet makes no claims except to be saying something which seems to him both agreeable and true. And as often as not it *is* both agreeable and true.

At least this can be said of the best of the earlier Georgian poetry and for the work of a very few of the newcomers in the later volumes, notably Edmund Blunden, who produced some of the most brilliant examples of this quiet and static poetry. But the impact of the war rocked the whole Georgian position very seriously and finally shattered it. It was difficult to fit the war into a walled garden and impossible to combine any longer agreeableness and truth. As might be expected, truth was the first to be sacrificed. In the 1916–17 collection John Freeman has a group of poems with normal Georgian titles—"Music Comes," "November Skies," "Discovery," "It Was the Lovely Moon," "Stone Trees," "The Pigeons," and a final one entitled "Happy Is England Now." The last is a war poem, the only war poem of the group, and it is written in exactly the same tone of gentle happiness in nature that characterizes the others.

> There is not anything more wonderful
> Than a great people moving towards the deep
> Of an unguessed and unfeared future; nor
> Is aught so dear of aught held dear before
> As the new passion stirring in their veins
> When the destroying Dragon wakes from sleep.
> Happy is England now as never yet! . . . .
>
> Whate'er was dear before is dearer now
> There's not a bird singing upon his bough
> But sings the sweeter in our English ears:
> There's not a nobleness of heart, hand, brain
> But shines the purer; happiest is England now
> In those that fight, and watch with pride and tears.

War has been brought—into the garden, and has become unrecognizable in the process. When we find a stanza like

> Happy is England in the brave that die
> For wrongs not hers and wrongs so sternly hers;
> Happy in those that give, give, and endure
> The pain that never the new years may cure;
> Happy in all her dark woods, green fields, towns,
> Her hills and rivers and her chafing sea:

—when we find a stanza like this, it becomes clear that the Georgian retreat is doomed. No such view of war could survive the facts of a long-drawn-out struggle; a meditative rusticity domiciling the western front among the lanes and fields of England has obviously gone the way from isolation to falsification. In the very next volume (1918–19) the poems of Siegfried Sassoon gave the lie to Freeman, and the game was up. It was up even without this attack, for the comparative unity of purpose and attitude which had underlain the first volumes began to disappear with the appearance of newcomers, and the rising challenge of other poets, not represented in the anthologies, made the Georgian volumes less and less representative of their age. The Georgian retrenchment had not lasted; the tide swirling up the beach with steady advance had broken down the children's pleasant forts of sand.

The prefatory note to the 1920–22 volume (which was to be the last) is querulous in tone:

When the fourth volume of this series was published three years ago, many of the critics who had up till then, as Horace Walpole said of God, been the dearest creatures in the world to me, took another turn. Not only did they very properly disapprove my choice of poems: they went on to write as if the Editor of *Georgian Poetry* were a kind of public functionary, like the President of the Royal Academy; and they asked—again, on this assumption, very properly—who was E. M. that he should bestow and withhold crowns and sceptres, and decide that this or that poet was or was not to count.

This indication of public criticism was of course to be expected. The Georgian experiment had begun before the war as an attempt to recapture decaying traditions, to mark time with faces turned away from the clock. It was an important experiment, and in some degree a successful one; but it could not hope to survive the war. The enthusiasm for the English tradition and the love of the English countryside which provided the main motivation were in themselves altogether laudable, but the post-war world demanded a great deal more than that, besides making it clear that the gardens of the Georgian poets had lost their protecting walls. Rupert Brooke, dying before he had time to understand the reality of the war, had remained to the end faithful to the garden. It is the fashion to sneer at Brooke, and charge that he ought to have known better; but at the time he died nobody in England knew better, and he, doubtless, would have learned like the others had he lived. His poetry is not, as the current criticism would have it, shallow or perverse: it is severely limited, but, so far as it goes, adequate and effective. He loved Grantchester, and Grantchester was a pleasant place. To deny him the right to express his affection with half-humorous nostalgia is purposeless and puritanical. Indeed, the puritan attitude to poetry has been growing of late, and critics have laid down what a man ought to feel. That is nonsense, and such an approach can yield no useful assessment of the Georgians. The situation can perhaps be more simply and more properly indicated by suggesting that when Brooke wrote

> Say, is there Beauty yet to find?
> And Certainty? and Quiet kind?
> Deep meadows yet, for to forget
> The lies, and truths, and pain? . . . . oh! yet
> Stands the Church clock at ten to three?
> And is there honey still for tea?

he assumed the probability of an affirmative answer. But by 1920 the answer was in the negative. The Georgian retrenchment collapsed when it became clear —as a result of the war and of the whole movement of European civilization—that tea had to be consumed without honey and the church clock had ticked on long past ten to three.

CHAPTER IV

WAR POETRY—THE IMAGISTS—POST-WAR
SATIRE—THE SITWELLS

THE reality of the great war came slowly into English poetry. After the spate of patriotic verse at the beginning of the war—ranging from the crude drum-beating of the journalistic poets to the meditations on the English countryside of the Georgians—there slowly appeared indications of a more realistic attitude. In the 1916–17 volume of *Georgian Poetry* appeared three war poems by Wilfred Wilson Gibson (whose war poetry, though standing apart from the rest of his work, is not dissimilar in quality) where for the first time something of the truth was told. In level, even tones concealing an irony more controlled but no less effective than that of Siegfried Sassoon, he described single incidents:

> I felt a sudden wrench—
> A trickle of warm blood—
> And found that I was sprawling in the mud
> Among the dead men in the trench.

Or, as in the poem "Lament," also in this volume, he rejects the facile consolation which had sufficed for John Freeman in his "Happy Is England Now":

> We who are left, how shall we look again
> Happily on the sun or feel the rain . . . . ?
> A bird among the rain-wet lilac sings—
> But we, how shall we turn to little things
> And listen to the birds and winds and streams
> Made holy by their dreams,
> Nor feel the heartbreak in the heart of things?

In the quietness of Gibson's war poetry lies much of its effect. He has no clear attitude; he cannot pause to think through what it all means, but he tells the truth in simple unadorned verse and leaves it at that. The irony emerges automatically, as it were:

> This bloody steel
> Has killed a man.
> I heard him squeal
> As on I ran.

The poems from which this verse is quoted did not appear in *Georgian Poetry*, nor indeed did any of Gibson's war poetry appear there apart from the three already referred to. Yet the whole sequence of thirty poems entitled *Battle* was written in 1914–15. There is little skill in these verses, but they are clearly etched and possess power:

> I lay an age and idly gazed at nothing
> Half-puzzled that I couldn't lift my head;
> And then somehow I knew that I was lying
> Among the other dead.

In the same volume of *Georgian Poetry* in which Gibson's three war poems appeared there were also printed several of Siegfried Sassoon's war poems. Sassoon was the first English poet to rebel with vigor and passion against the older tradition of war poetry, and he was one of the very few poets who expressed this mood continually and violently while the war was still in progress. The ironic note in his verse is not subdued, as it is in Gibson, but emphasized and shouted out loud. The poems published in the Georgian volume were more restrained than his verse published independently in *The Old Huntsman* (1917) and *Counter-attack*, but his characteristic tone is clearly heard:

> So Davies wrote: 'This leaves me in the pink.'
> Then scrawled his name: 'Your loving sweetheart, Willie.'
> With crosses for a hug. He'd had a drink
> Of rum and tea; and, though the barn was chilly,
> For once his blood ran warm; he had pay to spend . . . .
>
> And then he thought: tomorrow night we trudge
> Up to the trenches, and my boots are rotten.
> Five miles of stodgy clay and freezing sludge,
> And everything but wretchedness forgotten.
> To-night he's in the pink; but soon he'll die.
> And still the war goes on; *he* don't know why.

The note is perhaps more clearly heard in the poem "They," where the bishop's statement that "when the boys come back they will not be the same; for they have fought in a just cause" is put beside the boys' reply:

> 'We're none of us the same!' the boys reply.
> 'For George lost both his legs; and Bill's stone blind;
> Poor Jim's shot through the lungs and like to die;
> And Bert's gone syphilitic; you'll not find
> A chap who's served that hasn't found *some* change.'

This is a crude type of poetry, but it gets its point across with effective vigor. The tone becomes more aggressive in his later poems:

> Does it matter?—losing your sight? . . . .
> There's such splendid work for the blind;
> And people will always be kind,
> As you sit on the terrace remembering
> And turning your face to the light.

Or in these lines:

> Do you remember the stretcher cases lurching back
> With dying eyes and lolling heads, those ashen-grey
> Masks of the lads who once were keen and kind and gay?

Unlike Gibson, Sassoon continually expresses the underlying feeling that someone is to blame for it all— perhaps the smug civilians who cheer when troops march by on their way to embarkation, perhaps the "scarlet Majors at the base" who, "when the war is done and youth stone dead," will "toddle safely home and die—in bed." There is a terrible indignation here, but its direction is confused.

The quietest of all the war poems were written by Edmund Blunden, who saw the war against the background of daily pastoral life which it had interrupted (a mood frequent also in Gibson) and recorded with patient fidelity what he observed in those moments, as, for example, in "A Farm near Zillebeke":

> I stood in the yard of a house that must die,
> And still the black hame was stacked by the door,
> And harness hung there, and the dray waited by.
>
> Black clouds hid the moon, tears blinded me more..

Poems like this—"Battalion in Rest," "Vlamertinghe: Passing the Chateau, July 1917," "Rural Economy (1917)," "The Sentry's Mistake"—show a quality of philosophic observation rare in war poetry. Blunden has no thesis about the rights or wrongs of the war, he has no indignation, no wish to denounce. His dominant mood is simply one of sorrow, enhanced by the continual impingement on the present situation of pre-war memories of life and growth and peace. His war poetry has thus an elegiac quality entirely lacking in that of Sassoon. In all his poetry Blunden sounds the subdued elegiac note. He is one of the few English poets who have achieved some success in carrying the mood of the Georgians into the post-war

world. But his verse lacks vitality; it solves no problems, achieves none of that quick cutting to the heart
of things which some of his younger contemporaries,
using a more difficult and a more complex dialectic,
have on occasions managed. The meditations of a sensitive yet in some respects an academic mind, his work
does not achieve the vision which shifting values and
a worn-out medium demanded, and as a result most
of his poems lack that burning core and complete integration which we find in the poetry of those poets
who, wresting language to meet the urgency of their
own problems, by being "modern" produce what will
nevertheless have meaning and vitality for future generations.

Perhaps the best of all the poetry produced as a result of the war was written by Wilfred Owen, who was
born in 1893, three years before Blunden, and was
killed on November 4, 1918—exactly a week before the
Armistice—while endeavoring to get his company
across the Sambre Canal. Before the war he had begun
his career as poet largely under the influence of Keats.
But at this stage he was simply experimenting with
ways of handling language, learning his craft, disci-
plining himself. His war experiences found him with
no preconceived attitude; he was honest both as man
and as poet, and he waited to see what the war was
to mean for him and his poetry. He brought all his
powers of poetic expression—still at the experimental
stage—to his endeavor to find and to express the real
meaning of the situation in which he found himself.
He moved slowly from description to interpretation,
his earlier war poetry being concerned with adequate

expression of the facts and his later verse endeavoring to arrange the facts in some symbolic and significant pattern. A poem like "Exposure" or the fragment "Cramped in That Funnelled Hole" is simply descriptive, yet even here we can see the poet searching for a new handling of his medium which would give more urgency and effectiveness to his expression:

> Slowly our ghosts drag home: glimpsing the sunk fires, glozed
> With crusted dark-red jewels; crickets jingle there;
> For hours the innocent mice rejoice: the house is theirs;
> Shutters and doors, all closed: on us the doors are closed,—
> We turn back to our dying.

In these poems there is a careful originality in the use of adjectives and in the balancing of rhythms, and a deliberate use of half-rhymes instead of conventional rhyme, which indicates qualities possessed by Owen from the beginning—qualities which set him apart from the poets of the Georgian anthologies even before he turned to his characteristic kind of war poetry. As interpretation succeeded description in his poetry of the war, Owen gradually developed the theme suggested in his draft of a preface to a projected volume of poems found among his papers after his death:

This book is not about heroes. English poetry is not yet fit to speak of them.

Nor is it about deeds, or lands, nor anything about glory, honour, might, majesty, dominion, or power, except War.

My subject is War and the pity of War.

The Poetry is in the Pity.

Yet these elegies are to this generation in no sense consolatory. They may be to the next. All a poet can do to-day is to warn. That is why the true Poets must be truthful.[1]

[1] *The Poems of Wilfred Owen*, edited with a memoir and notes by Edmund Blunden (London, 1931).

It is not easy to see exactly what Owen meant in this hastily written draft of a preface. He seems to be saying that his war poems are not concerned with any of the subjects conventionally associated with war, nor is he concerned with mere poetizing, in the manner of so many of the Georgians. When he says that English poetry is not yet fit to speak of heroes, he seems to mean that the real nature of the heroism called forth by the war could not be adequately expressed in any of the traditional ways nor in the poetic medium in its present state; the truth was difficult to discover and even more difficult to communicate. When he asserts that "above all, I am not concerned with Poetry," he is obviously rejecting any self-conscious aesthetic aim: he was concerned with expressing adequately the truth as he saw it, as he had experienced it, and, for him, adequately implied poetically. "My subject is War and the pity of War. The Poetry is in the Pity" indicates that the meaning of the war experience, as he had come to grasp it, lies in its sheer pity, its futility, its waste. By expressing that truth his poetry might become a warning. But it could have no other moral. For himself, he was expressing the essential reality of the situation as he saw it, and that was his whole aim. If in achieving this aim he also achieved a propagandist effect—in the sense that the truth carries its own message—he would not repudiate that effect or deny that he had foreseen it.

He did not immediately arrive at the interpretation that is summed up in his phrase, "The Poetry is in the Pity." After his early descriptive verses he attempted some in Sassoon's style, in which he was concerned simply to attack false attitudes to the war:

> If in some smothered dreams you too could pace
> Behind the wagon that we flung him in,
> And watch the white eyes writhing in his face,
> His hanging face, like a devil's sick of sin;
> If you could hear, at every jolt, the blood
> Come gargling from the froth-corrupted lungs,
> Bitter as the cud
> Of vile, incurable sores on innocent tongues,—
> My friend, you would not tell with such high zest
> To children ardent for some desperate glory,
> The old Lie: Dulce et decorum est
> Pro patria mori.

This is fairly crude verse, where the passion is expressing itself in simple rhetoric. But Owen soon moved to a calmer kind of interpretation:

> Whether his deeper sleep lie shaded by the shaking
> Of great wings, and the thoughts that hung the stars,
> High-pillowed on calm pillows of God's making
> Above these clouds . . . .
> —Or whether yet his thin and sodden head
> Confuses more and more with the low mould,
> His hair being one with the grey grass
> And finished fields of autumns that are old . . . .
> Who knows? Who hopes? Who troubles? Let it pass!
> He sleeps. He sleeps less tremulous, less cold,
> Than we who must awake, and waking, say Alas!

Owen's progress was not, however, a simple one from satiric to contemplative war poems. The violent anger that breaks through "Mental Cases," "Disabled." and other poems is that of a man who has not resigned himself to express merely the pity of war, but who is equally anxious to convey its horror, its terror, and its cruelty. But in the midst of these we begin to find more disciplined verse sounding a profounder note, poems whose simple elegiac quality indicates Owen's progress toward the ideal indicated in the draft preface. The "Anthem for Doomed Youth" impresses by its simple opening question

> What passing-bells for those who die as cattle?

and the slow and plangent answer:

> No mockeries for them from prayers or bells,
>   Nor angry voice of mourning save the choirs,—
> The shrill demented choirs of wailing shells;
>   And bugles calling for them from sad shires.
>
> What candles may be held to speed them all?
>   Not in the hands of boys, but in their eyes
> Shall shine the holy glimmers of good-byes.
>   The pallor of girls' brows shall be their pall;
> Their flowers the tenderness of silent minds,
> And each slow dusk a drawing-down of blinds.

This, perhaps the best of Owen's poems, is, for all its simplicity, a highly organized piece of work. The series of multiple contrasts set going between wartime life and peacetime life, between the battle front and domestic scenes at home, by the careful choice and arrangement of images shows a grasp of poetic structure that proclaims the mature poet. The precise function in the poem of the term "cattle" (with its double suggestion of wartime horror and peacetime farming linking with similar combinations and contrasts throughout the poem), the effect of the phrase "sad shires" (with its suggestion of a denuded pastoral England sending forth its sons to die amid foreign horror), the whole weaving of contrasts and correspondences that achieve effectiveness by a deliberately multiple relationship between the two (parallels fading into contrasts, and vice versa, thus adding to the depth and poignancy of the poem) are questions that could be discussed at length had we space to pause at a single poem.

The incomplete "Strange Meeting" can stand beside "Anthem for Doomed Youth" as expressing with calm and terrible effectiveness "the pity of war." Unfinished as it is, "Strange Meeting" yet has a certain completeness: there is the story of his meeting the strange friend in Hell, the other's discourse on "the undone years, the hopelessness" common to both of them, and the final recognition and resolution:

> I am the enemy you killed, my friend . . . .
> Let us sleep now.

The poem moves smoothly to its sudden and hopeless close (for the close *is* hopeless: there is no way of regaining the life that both were prevented from living and utilizing; the only good left is oblivion for both). There is complete technical mastery here, a consistent and careful use of half-rhymes, a subtle and well-handled imagery. There can be no doubt that Owen was developing rapidly, seeking out new attitudes, mastering new subtleties of technique, responding to experience with that adaptability both as man and as poet which distinguishes the genuine artist from the talented pedant.

Just what the war of 1914–18 did to English poetry is very difficult to determine. Of course it produced war poetry, a poetry which changed its character as the realities of war became better known. It probably helped to make the Georgians look out of date some years before they otherwise would have, though it is difficult to be certain of this. One specific and tangible result was that it killed off a great number of promising poets, chief among whom was Wilfred Owen, just getting into his stride when he met his death. Isaac Rosenberg, born in 1890, a poet of strange power and great promise, was killed in April, 1918, leaving behind him a fairly slender output of poetry, but sufficient to mark his vigor and originality. Francis Ledwidge, one of the early Georgian poets whose nature poetry is characterized by a thin romantic delicacy, was killed in 1917 at the age of twenty-six.

Among the poets killed in the war was Edward Thomas, who came comparatively late to the writing of poetry, encouraged by Robert Frost on the latter's arrival in England in 1912. His meditative nature poetry is Georgian with a difference; it has none of the obvious or trivial qualities associated with the Georgians, for Thomas cultivated a type of what might be called metaphysical observation which enabled him to infuse into a meticulous account of an event in nature a certain unexpected thought or vision which reflects a strange light around the whole poem. His imagery, when examined image by image, seems to derive simply from careful observation, yet on reading any of the poems we are aware of some unexpected meaning emerging from the imagery, though it is difficult to explain how or why. The poem "The Gallows" is a typical example of this simplicity which results in the final emergence of a strange vision:

> There was a weasel lived in the sun
> With all his family,
> Till a keeper shot him with a gun

And hung him on a tree,
Where he swings in the wind and rain,
In the sun and in the snow,
Without pleasure, without pain,
On the dead oak tree bough.

Even from this single opening stanza we can appreciate something of the *distilled* quality of Thomas' poetry. The often and justly admired "Tears" illustrates to an unusual degree the strange visionary quality which Thomas can distil out of images in themselves ordinary:

It seems I have no tears left. They should have fallen—
Their ghosts, if tears have ghosts, did fall—that day
When twenty hounds streamed by me, not yet combed out
But still all equals in their rage of gladness
Upon the scent, made one, like a great dragon
In Blooming Meadows that bends towards the sun
And once bore hops . . . .

Accepting the Georgian narrowing of subject matter, Thomas nevertheless succeeds in revitalizing a worn tradition simply by this quality of original vision which he embodies in his poetry not so much as a result of his imagery as of the manner in which he organizes it. Thomas was killed at Arras in 1917, just when his original style seemed to be reaching its full development. He would have founded no school, for he was an individual poet and in a sense a backward-looking poet; yet, had he survived the war, he might have produced some arresting poetry in his maturity—for, though born in 1878, he was still very young as a poet at his death.

Neither the Georgians nor the various kinds of war poets exhausted the poetry of the period. In addition to the Georgian attempt to preserve the tradition by attenuating it (by pastoralism, by quiet and limited realism, by meditation), there was the more violent and breezy traditionalism of such writers as Chesterton and Belloc, who, in ballad rhythms and in other kinds of swinging verse, expressed hearty love for England, her institutions, her countryside, her past. The cheerful beery quality of Chesterton and the not dissimilar (though more satiric) flavor of Belloc's patriotism indicate traditionalism on the defensive. The defense was conducted with a certain intelligence and a great deal of noise, and when the tumult and the shouting died two rather pathetic figures could be seen sitting with foaming tankards of beer on a rustic bench outside an English country tavern with their eyes turned eagerly to the rolling plains and the winding lanes of England, and their minds cast wistfully back to a heavily tinted Middle Ages.

But more important for the future of English poetry were attempts to reshape the poetic medium, either by limitation or by expansion. The most important attempt of the former sort was that represented by the Imagist movement, which endeavored to effect a serious narrowing of the technique and language of poetry in a desire to escape the flabbiness which was the natural accompaniment of attempts to practice in a worn-out tradition. The Imagists strove consciously to write poetry in accordance with a strict and carefully elaborated theory. The theory, however, was not revolutionary or even new; in its various statements it sounds like a description of the writing habits of almost all great poets. But though the theory itself was commonplace, its articulation with such precision developed in response to an attitude toward poetry and toward art generally which was developing in England and in the United States contemporaneously with the Georgian movement and which had a great deal of influence on the progress of poetry in both countries. It was an inherently conservative movement, whose aim was similar to that of the Georgians though the means used to achieve this aim was wholly different. The Georgian retrenchment took the form of quietest retreat: the Imagist retrenchment concerned itself with language rather than with attitudes, and its main contribution was technical.

The origins of the Imagist movement are manifold—French, classical, and oriental—but it is more important to determine what these poets were trying to do and why than to list the authors who influenced them.[2] Their aim was limitation and precision; in general, they conceived their art to be "classical" rather than "romantic," and the intellectual background of the movement was supplied, though in an indirect fashion, by T. E. Hulme. Of Hulme's general philosophical position and his protest against romanticism, naturalism, humanism, and utopianism we shall say something later; at the moment we are concerned only with his contribution to the Imagist movement. This contribution was made largely by his insistence that poetry should be "dry and hard," his repudiation of the kind of romantic verse which brings in "the emotions that are grouped round the word infinite," his advocacy of

[2] Readers who are interested in the origins of imagism are referred to the first chapter of Glenn Hughes's *Imagism and the Imagists* (Stanford University: Stanford University Press; London: Oxford University Press, 1931).

a classicism in art which implied the precise and disciplined use of visual images in poetry "in order to get the exact curve of the thing." This precise use of visual images represented a tendency toward poetic discipline which was to be found emerging at the beginning of the second decade of the twentieth century among a variety of poets. It was only gradually that these poets came together to found a school, and when they did come together their asssociation did not last very long. But their achievement remained influential in English and American poetry.

The Georgians tried to save the tradition by limitation of subject matter, and often achieved only wateriness. The Imagists sought the same end by limitation of technique, achieving hardness and precision even if these qualities were often accompanied by triviality. The movement was a sort of tightening of the belt, a cutting of losses, to keep English poetry from perishing from looseness and thin eclecticism. It aimed at what was after all a surface art, an impressionism which depended on no convictions: insisting on an ordinary vocabulary used with an extraordinary exactness, on *vers libre* rhythms if and when they most adequately represented the mood of the poet, on complete freedom in choice of subject matter, on the presentation of exact images, on hardness and clarity, and on concentration (which last they believed to be "the very essence of poetry"), they repudiated by implication not only Matthew Arnold's criterion of "high seriousness" but all concepts of significance in subject matter or ideas, all aspects of poetic structure except the simple one of relation between images, and all aspects of language except carefulness of denotation and exactness of visual suggestion. They escaped altogether from the world of values, in an endeavor to free themselves from the disturbance caused by disintegrating traditions and ideals. They were indeed one of the first groups of artists who endeavored to solve the problems faced by art in a world of dissolving values by concentrating entirely on technique. The Georgians retained a carefully selected number of the old values, though often in a rather halfhearted way; the Imagists tried to cut free entirely.

The Imagist poets came to the movement through various channels. Hulme himself, whose imagism was the result of his classicism and his insistence on hardness, clarity, and restraint, produced only five poems,[3] which were published in 1912 as a supplement to Ezra Pound's *Ripostes* as "The Complete Poetical Works of T. E. Hulme." This would probably have remained the extent of his poetical output even if he had not been killed while serving as artilleryman in Flanders in September, 1917, for his attention was turning more and more to philosophy and criticism: his interests were always more theoretical than practical. Hulme's five poems are, however, typical Imagist productions and served as a model for other poets of the group. The poems are only a few lines long and contain such careful and precise images as these:

> I walked abroad,
> And saw the ruddy moon lean over a hedge
> Like a red-faced farmer . . . .

[3] Three other poems by Hulme are printed in Michael Roberts' *T. E. Hulme* (London: Faber & Faber, 1938), Appen. I.

Oh, God, make small
The old star-eaten blanket of the sky,
That I may fold it round me and in comfort lie.

Now pass I to the final river
Ignominiously, in a sack, without sound,
As any peeping Turk to the Bosphorus.

These short poems contain precision of imagery and
nothing else; they communicate visual sensation with
great effectiveness, but the experience expressed has
neither organization nor totality. The images are independent of one another; each has validity and impressiveness as a unit, but they bear no organic relation to a single whole. Imagist poems tend to be dry
in more senses than Hulme intended; they have not the
"dampness" to which Hulme objected in romantic
poetry, but they have a great emptiness. We re-read
these verses in the hope that the heart of the poem will
reveal itself, but it never does,· for there is no heart.
It is like approaching the shelves of an impressive and
well-stocked library and finding on inspection that the
books are dummies.

Ezra Pound was largely responsible for getting the
Imagist movement into shape and giving it some coherence, though he left the group in 1914, when Amy
Lowell took over. Pound had had contacts with
Hulme, but he had also reached a position similar to
Hulme's independently. Influenced first by Provençal
poetry and, to a lesser degree, by the Latin and Greek
lyrical poets, and later by the classical poetry of China
and Japan, Pound was writing poetry that fitted him
admirably to be both spokesman for the Imagists and

one of their chief practitioners. *Ripostes* contains stanzas like these:

> Golden rose the house, in the portal I saw
> thee, a marvel, carven in subtle stuff, a
> portent. Life died down in the lamp and flickered,
> caught at the wonder.[4]

> Tree you are,
> Moss you are,
> You are violets with wind above them.
> A child—*so* high—you are,
> And all this is folly to the world.[5]

In later volumes, *Lustra* (1916, but written earlier) and *Cathay* (1915), the Chinese influence results in a very careful imagism:

> The petals fall in the fountain,
>   the orange-coloured rose leaves . . . .

> The narrow streets cut into the wide highway
>   at Choan,
> Dark oxen, white horses,
>   drag on the seven coaches with outriders . . . .

> The red and green kingfishers
>   flash between the orchids and clover,
> One bird casts its gleam on another. . . . .

Pound was not the only one whose imagism was encouraged by Chinese and Japanese example. John Gould Fletcher, the American Imagist, was similarly influenced, both by Japanese pictorial art and by the precision and economy of the Japanese verse forms *tanka* and *hokku*. Indeed, there was a fairly widespread interest in oriental art both in England and in America at this time; while Hulme, taking over Wilhelm Wor-

---

[4] From "Apparuit."   [5] From "A Girl."

ringer's view of the nature of oriental culture, looked to that art to illustrate his ideal of classicism.

The colorful and eclectic experimentalism of the American-born Ezra Pound was something different from the quiet Hellenism of Richard Aldington and H. D. (Hilda Doolittle), yet all three were led to imagism. H. D. also hailed from America, and soon after her arrival in Europe in 1911 she became associated with Aldington in writing *vers libre* on Greek subjects. In the second issue of *Poetry: A Magazine of Verse*, November, 1912, there was a group of three poems by Aldington and the following note about their author:

Mr. Richard Aldington is a young English poet, one of the "Imagistes," a group of ardent Hellenists who are pursing interesting experiments in *vers libre;* trying to attain in English certain subtleties of cadence of the kind which Mallarmé and his followers studied in French.

This short note illustrates something of the confusion with which the origin of imagism was surrounded. Actually, the experiments with "certain subtleties of cadence" were not the distinguishing feature of imagism—a consideration which the very title of the movement would suggest.

Pound, who was foreign correspondent for Harriet Monroe's *Poetry*, wrote an account of the state of English poetry from London in December, 1912, which appeared in the next month's issue. He remarked of the *Imagistes* (the final *e* had not yet been dropped, and the word was still italicized) that "they are in opposition to the numerous and unassembled writers who busy themselves with dull and interminable effusions, and who seem to think that a man can write a good long poem before he learns to write a good short one, or even before he learns to produce a good single line." The Imagists were all for the short poem—in which they resembled the nineteenth-century romantics more than they realized, for the romantic view placed the short lyric at the top of the hierarchy of literary forms, as opposed to the eminence given by the neoclassic critics to the epic. Imagism was essentially a conservative movement, though, like so many conservative movements, it sailed under a revolutionary flag.

In the same issue of *Poetry* in which this article of Pound's appeared there were four poems signed *H. D.*, "*Imagiste*," under the general title, "Verses, Translations, and Reflections from 'The Anthology.'" Of these the editor's note said: "Her sketches from the Greek are not offered as exact translations, or as in any sense finalities, but as experiments in delicate and elusive cadences, which attain sometimes a haunting beauty." In the same number Ezra Pound was saying that the watchword of the Imagists was Precision. The contradiction between precision and elusiveness was not so great as might seem, for H. D. sought precision in capturing elusive images. One might say that the Imagists were concerned with being precise about things that did not matter and were not made to seem to matter except as precise individual perceptions, linked to no central idea, related to no scheme of values. H. D.'s individual images are effective:

> Apples on the small trees
> Are hard,
> Too small,
> Too late ripened
> By a desperate sun
> That struggles through sea-mist.

This is a pleasing surface art, showing skill and vision but, like all Imagist poetry, lacking "the shaping spirit of imagination." The fault, to express it in formal terms, is structural. We do not complain because the subject is not "significant" but because it is not given significance through organization. Hulme remarked in one of his essays: "It isn't the scale or kind of emotion produced that decides, but this one fact: Is there any real zest in it? Did the poet have an actually realized visual object before him in which he delighted? It doesn't matter if it were a lady's shoe or the starry heavens." We would agree with this, yet this is not the sum of the matter. Hulme, like the Imagists whom he influenced, was naïve about the nature of poetic form. Clarity and precision of the individual image provide only one criterion; the richness and wholeness of texture provided by the adequate integration of the separate images is a criterion equally important, but one neglected both by Hulme and by the Imagists. No wonder, then, that they preferred the short poem, in which the necessity of integration is not so pressing nor the task of integrating so difficult as in a longer work.

A complete statement of the critical position of the Imagists, written by F. S. Flint, appeared in *Poetry* for March, 1913. Flint had come into contact with Hulme and came to imagism through an interest in French Symbolism. In this statement, however, Flint speaks of the Imagists as an observer, and he probably got his information from Pound. He noted three rules which the Imagists observed:

1. Direct treatment of the "thing," whether subjective or objective

2. To use absolutely no word that did not contribute to the presentation
3. As regarding rhythm: to compose in sequence of the musical phrase, not in sequence of a metronome

Pound accompanied this statement with "A Few Don'ts by an Imagiste," which included such pieces of advice as, "Use no superfluous words, no adjective, which does not reveal something"; "Go in fear of abstractions"; "Let the candidate fill his mind with the finest cadences he can discover, preferably in a foreign language so that the meaning of the words may be less likely to divert his attention from the movement"; "Consider the way of the scientists rather than the way of an advertising agent"; "If you want the gist of the matter go to Sappho, Villon, Heine when he is in the vein, Gautier when he is not too frigid; or, if you have not the tongues, seek out the leisurely Chaucer." The Imagist movement was now properly launched, with keen practitioners and a critical theory. What strikes us most about the critical theory, as enunciated by Pound, is its extreme naïveté. To lay down rules of this kind for all who wished to write good poetry was to confess to some kind of failure in the poetic tradition. And it might well be argued that it was a failure of the tradition which produced both the Georgians and the Imagists.

The Imagists in England published chiefly in the *Egoist*, which was founded in the beginning of 1914, with Aldington on the editorial staff. The contributing poets included Aldington himself, Pound, H. D., F. S. Flint, John Gould Fletcher, Amy Lowell, and D. H. Lawrence. Lawrence was an Imagist *malgré lui* and accepted his position among the group without any great interest in its creed or principles. He wrote as he had always written, and the Imagists accepted him as a brother. T. S. Eliot also contributed to the *Egoist*, and though never officially an Imagist his work was considerably influenced by Imagist principles. (Eliot became editor of the paper in 1917 and remained such until its demise in December, 1919.)

In March, 1914, appeared *Des Imagistes: An Anthology*, a rather precious compilation which bore no editor's name or explanation of any kind. It was Pound's idea, conceived largely in order to boost the work of Aldington and H. D., but other poets were included, though to a less degree, including Pound himself and F. S. Flint and one poem each from seven other writers including Amy Lowell and James Joyce. After this publication Pound lost interest in the movement, and the leadership was assumed by Amy Lowell, who collected a group of the faithful around her and brought out three Imagist anthologies in the United States in 1915, 1916, and 1917. The contributors were Aldington, H. D., John Gould Fletcher, F. S. Flint, D. H. Lawrence, and Amy Lowell herself. Of these, Aldington, Flint, and Lawrence were English and the other three American, at least in origin.

There was a lot of quite un-Imagist poetry in the three Imagist anthologies (*Some Imagist Poets* was the title of each volume). Quite a lot of Aldington's verses was the poetry of ideas, not of images. In "Childhood," for example, and in "Vicarious Atonement," there are not many images and what there are are not important: the meaning is carried by the verbs and often by abstract nouns ("The bitterness, the misery, the wretchedness of childhood"). D. H. Lawrence's poems are fables, Imagist neither in form nor content. Fletcher keeps more accurately to the Imagist program with careful and picturesque descriptions:

> Yellow melon flowers
> Crawl between the withered peach-trees;
> A date-palm throws its heavy fronds of steel
> Against the scoured metallic sky.

Flint keeps the rule, too, but with a tendency to drift into a conventional romantic imagery suggestive of Shelley or Rossetti. Amy Lowell had a surfeit of images, and her contributions are fluent and copious, containing skilfully handled pictures following each other rapidly but lacking discipline and tightness. H. D. is the most successful of all: she keeps the Imagist rules and manages to produce highly effective little poems of great surface brilliance. This is as far as imagism can go:

> Weed, moss-weed,
> root tangled in sand,
> sea-iris, brittle flower,
> one petal like a shell
> is broken,
> and you print a shadow
> like a thin twig.

The last of the three Imagist anthologies appeared in 1917, by which time the limitations of the movement had become apparent to the Imagists themselves, who turned to wider fields. A nostalgic *Imagist Anthology, 1930* was published thirteen years later (it was Aldington's idea) with poems from those who contributed both to Pound's initial anthology and to Amy Lowell's three volumes.

And so the second attempt at retrenchment came to an end. It cannot be said to have failed any more than the Georgians can be said to have failed. Neither group produced the greatest poetry, but each contributed something. The gentle pastoralism of the better Georgians is a modification of the pastoral tradition, a delicate achievement which is real if slight; while the careful discipline of the Imagists at their best not only produced some excellent minor lyrics but also made an important contribution to later poetry. T. S. Eliot's skill in manipulating images owes something to the Imagists, with whom he was associated at one time. Eliot contributes a highly developed sense of form to the Imagist visual sensitivity and becomes a brilliant poetic technician.

The poets were turning to larger themes. Retrenchment and isolation were not going to work in the post-war world; the poet would have to come out into the open and take stock. Aldington ceased to be merely an Imagist and, in direct contradiction of the Imagist canons, produced a long poem, *A Fool i' the Forest* (1925) in which he tried to come to grips with the contemporary situation. Already three years before this T. S. Eliot had published *The Waste Land*, an attempt to observe and pass judgment on the modern situation. In 1911 the English poets seemed to be seeking nothing more than a slow and quiet death in a familiar English setting, writing verses to the end. This elegiac note was not to be heard in 1920. The confusion, the hysteria, the emptiness of the post-war world destroyed

the position of Georgians and of Imagists alike. The
new mood was expressed at first indirectly, in poems of
sophisticated weariness, in satire, in self-conscious attempts to return to a previous age, in hysterical stunts
and carefully fostered artificialities; in fact, every kind
of sublimation was to be found before Eliot endeavored
to express directly the mood of his generation. *Wheels*,
an anthology edited by Edith Sitwell which appeared
annually from 1916 until 1921, provides one of the
first indirect expressions of this mood. More deliberately anti-Georgian than the Imagists ever were, the
contributors to *Wheels* repudiated the traditionalism
of the Georgians and sublimated their own sense of
decay into verses sometimes bizarre, sometimes satiri-
cal, sometimes artificial. Beneath it all lay a subdued
hysteria.

The first volume of *Wheels* opens with a poem by
Nancy Cunard which is wholly representative in
theme and tone of the dominant mood of the volume:

> I sometimes think that all our thoughts are wheels
> Rolling for ever through the painted world,
> Moved by the cunning of a thousand clowns
> Dressed paper-wise, with blatant rounded masks,
> That take their multi-coloured caravans
> From place to place, and act and leap and sing,
> Catching the spinning hoops when cymbals clash.
> And one is dressed as Fate, and one as Death,
> The rest that represent Love, Joy and Sin,
> Join hands in solemn stage-learned ecstasy,
> While Folly beats a drum with golden pegs,
> And mocks that shrouded jester called Despair.

A picturesque verbal clowning with a feeling of emptiness underneath is to be found frequently in all the

volumes of *Wheels*. There is a recurrent *commedia dell'
arte* note, a deliberate artificiality, colorful masks and
studied gestures, but underlying it all there is an implied criticism, sometimes a suggestion of despair,
sometimes even of hysteria. We get it in an obvious
manner in Osbert Sitwell's "Twentieth Century Harli-
quinade":

> The pantomime of life is near its close:
> The stage is strewn with ends and bits of things,
> With mortals maim'd or crucified, and left
> To gape at endless horror through eternity.

We get it in the tortured yet sophisticated contributions of Aldous Huxley, notably in the prose-poems
of the 1918 volume.

> But I happened to look inwards among the machinery of our
> roundabout, and there I saw a slobbering cretin grinding at a
> wheel and sweating as he ground and grinding eternally. And
> when I perceived that he was the author of all our speed and that
> the music was of his making, that everything depended on his
> grinding wheel, I thought I would like to get off. But we were
> going too fast.

For the most part, *Wheels* presents the Waste Land in
cap and bells. Beneath the glitter, the decoration, the
surface color, the ingenious playing with words, lies
the grinning skull. Even where the horror or the dis-
gust seems to be entirely absent the deliberate artificiality indicates the look averted from life. And sometimes the Waste Land atmosphere is not disguised at
all, but expressed openly and wearily, as in Iris Tree's
"Disenchantment" (in the 1919 *Wheels*):

> There is a purpose in Heaven,
> But for me
> Nothing.

Yet the Sitwells themselves (who are the main contributors to *Wheels*) can hardly be classed as Waste Land poets, whatever the ultimate implications of their work. All three—Edith, Osbert, and Sacheverell— are highly cultured and sophisticated writers with a strong sense of family tradition. But their culture and their sense of tradition have nothing to take hold on in an age of disintegration, and the result is that they use the material provided by their culture as colored counters to play with or, as in the case of Osbert, turn to a satire which, while both fierce and elegant, seems to be a little vague about what it is attacking. The origin of Osbert's satire is to be found in the frustration of culture implied in post-war civilization, but his satiric emotion, seeking an "objective correlative," finds specific and less fundamental objects of attack in modern politics and social behavior. It is a type of satire where the emotion comes first and then seeks a victim on which to vent it. This is a feature of much of the satire of the immediate post-war years: the satiric mood was profound, because it arose out of the modern dilemma which is itself profound, yet the subject was often trivial in comparison with the (often unconscious) origin of the bitterness which the poet sought to express. The revival of satire in the 1920's in the work of Osbert Sitwell, Siegfried Sassoon, Humbert Wolfe, and others is due to this cause and is of this general nature.

The influences on the Sitwells were manifold. Seventeenth- and eighteenth-century culture, baroque art, Chinese classical poetry and painting (at least in the case of Sacheverell), the French Symbolists, the draw ings of Aubrey Beardsley, and their own family tradition all helped to form their writing. The deliberate confusion of the senses shown by Edith Sitwell, the highly personal rococo images, the painted artificiality, the playfulness alternating with a half-suppressed grimness, the dream quality hovering between farce and nightmare, the marshaling of bright and brittle phrases with deliberate disregard of their relation to each other, the carefully fantastic situations, the tom-tom rhythms, the preference for geometric rather than natural form, the clowning, the mockery, the individuality—all these features of Edith Sitwell's poetry suggest a culture that has lost its roots and its normal function and as a result is being used as a quarry from which to dig up colored counters that are tossed into the air with the skill of an expert conjuror yet in a mood of suppressed hysteria. The art of Gertrude Stein, with its use of language as counters and its astonishing pragmatism (a rose is a rose is a rose), seems to have a similar origin to that of Edith Sitwell. In an age when culture seemed to have lost its roots, its flowers were arranged in artificial bunches in drawing-room vases instead of being allowed to grow in the soil: cut flowers in the Waste Land.

CHAPTER V

T. E. HULME AND T. S. ELIOT

THE revival of the heroic couplet by satirists such as Osbert Sitwell, Humbert Wolfe, and Roy Campbell was part of a revival of interest in the eighteenth century. Throughout the long heyday of English romanticism eighteenth-century poetry had been frowned on as shallow and artificial, bound by "rules" and thus not genuinely "poetic"; and it was not until the second decade of the twentieth century that a reaction to this view became apparent. This reaction had several causes. The formalism of the eighteenth century appealed to those who wished to return to some comfortable discipline and to escape from a literature becoming daily more confused about its values and more uncertain about its aims. One could escape from the confusion by a simple pragmatism (Gertrude Stein), by a return to an older discipline, or by an attempt to solve the problems of the contemporary world and to write according to the terms of your solution. The younger English poets of the 1930's chose the last of these three methods; nevertheless, their approach to poetry was in some degree influenced by those who chose the second. This second group was limited in numbers, and the expression of its views was never widely read. But its emergence was significant and its influence important. Its first and perhaps its greatest champion was T. E. Hulme, whose influence on the Imagists we have already noted. Hulme's influence on the Imagists was superficial, however, compared to that which his view of poetry, culture, and tradition and the relation between these three had on a group of critics of the period and in particular on one poet and critic—T. S. Eliot.

To what extent Eliot was influenced by Hulme, to what extent their thought moved independently along parallel lines, is a question not very easy to determine and not of any great importance. Eliot had no personal relations with Hulme but seems to have read and admired such of his work as was published: there can be no doubt that Eliot's later criticism owes some of its most essential features to Hulme. When he tells us, for example, that "with the disappearance of the idea of Original Sin . . . . the human beings presented to us both in poetry and in prose fiction to-day . . . . tend to become less and less real,"[1] he is echoing the main thought of Hulme's analysis of romanticism in his preface to his translation of Sorel's *Reflections on Violence*. Indeed, Hulme's views on classicism, on religion, on liberalism, are constantly repeated by Eliot in his later critical writing.

The important point, however, is not the degree to which Eliot's views were influenced by Hulme but the nature of the beliefs they shared. Both writers attack romantic individualism, liberalism, and, to a certain degree, democracy. Hulme expresses one aspect of

[1] *After Strange Gods: A Primer of Modern Heresy* (London and New York, 1934), p. 42.

this view with clarity and precision in his article on "Mr. Epstein and the Critics":

> I do think that there is a certain general state of mind which has lasted from the Renaissance till now, with what is, in reality, very little variation. . . . . It is perhaps enough to say that, taking at first the form of the "humanities," it has in its degeneracy taken the form of a belief in "Progress" and the rest of it. It was in its way a fairly consistent system, but it is probably at the moment breaking up. . . . . I feel, myself, a repugnance towards the *Weltanschauung* (as distinct from the technical part) of all philosophy since the Renaissance. In comparison with what I can vaguely call the religious attitude, it seems to me to be trivial.[2]

Later in the same article, quoting with disapproval a critic of Epstein who had complained of the latter's lack of "modern feeling," Hulme exclaims: "Modern feeling be damned! As if it were not the business of every honest man to clean the world of these sloppy dregs of the Renaissance." With this post-Renaissance habit of mind Hulme identifies the romanticism which springs from Rousseau, which revolves round the central proposition that "man is by nature wonderful, of unlimited powers, and if hitherto has not appeared so, it is because of external obstacles and fetters, which it should be the main business of social politics to remove." The opposite conception, which is Hulme's (and Eliot's) is "the conviction that a man is by nature bad or limited, and can consequently only accomplish anything of value by disciplines, ethical, heroic or political. In other words, it believes in Original Sin." And Hulme concludes: "We may define Romantics, then, as all those who do not believe in the Fall of Man."[3]

[2] *New Age*, December 25, 1913.
[3] "The Translator's Preface to Sorel's 'Reflections on Violence,' " *New Age*, October 14, 1915, p. 570.

Hulme's philosophical position was more elastic and more many-sided than these extracts would seem to suggest: he combined a strong anti-romanticism with an anti-rationalism derived largely from Bergson, a vague religious attitude with a strong vein of cynicism, a pragmatism in politics combined with a species of proto-fascism derived in part from the French Syndicalist, Georges Sorel, and from (to use Hulme's own phrase) "the brilliant group of writers connected with *L'Action française.*" In applying these views to criticism, he related the romantic individualist view, which he rejected, to naturalistic art, and the "religious" classical view to abstract art.

Eliot has not Hulme's philosophical eclecticism, and a fair number of Hulme's ideas find no reflection in Eliot's writing; but both writers share some very important and influential beliefs. Hulme's identification of classicism with anti-humanism and his confidence that "the humanist tradition is breaking up"[4] represented an association of concepts which was not accepted by later critics; for, paradoxically, Hulme's *literary* classicism was adopted by a new type of humanist. Hulme would have been surprised to see Irving Babbitt and Paul Elmer More sharing his classicism yet calling themselves humanists. Eliot was aware of the ambiguities involved in the term "humanist" and in his essays on the subject endeavors "to distinguish the functions of true Humanism from those imposed upon it by zealots." He explains:

I wish to distinguish sharply . . . . between what seems to me the correct and *necessarily* vague Humanism, and what T. E.

[4] *Speculations* (1924), p. 55.

Hulme means by Humanism in his notes in *Speculations*. I agree with what Hulme says; and I am afraid that many modern Humanists are explicitly or implicitly committed to the view which Hulme denounces; and that they are, in consequence, men of the Renaissance rather than men of our own time. For instance, Hulme gives as one characteristic of the Humanist (in his sense) the "refusal to believe any longer in the radical imperfection of either Man or Nature." I cannot help feeling that Mr Foerster and even Mr Babbitt are nearer to the view of Rousseau than they are to the religious view. . . . . It is to the immense credit of Hulme that he found out for himself that there is an *absolute* to which Man can never attain. . . . .[5]

And Eliot goes on to quote with approval Hulme's statement that "I hold the religious conception of values to be right, the humanist wrong" and his stress on the importance of "dogmas like that of Original Sin, which are the closest expression of the categories of the religious attitude."

What is happening here is a much more fundamental rejection of the nineteenth-century tradition than that represented by the return to the heroic couplet and the rehabilitation of the eighteenth century which we have already noted. This is the rejection of the tolerant humanism of Montaigne in favor of Pascal's anti-humanist religion, and the Montaigne tradition had governed western European thought almost uninterruptedly since the Renaissance. It is true that the acceptance of the Pascal view which we find in Hulme and Eliot did not represent any general intellectual movement; even if we include scholastic and Neo-Thomist currents (which Hulme would have had little sympathy with, though Eliot sympathizes), it remains

[5] "Second Thoughts on Humanism," *Selected Essays, 1917–1932* (New York, 1932), p. 401.

a small minority movement. Yet though we are not dealing here with a universal repudiation of a traditional habit of mind and are considering the work of a small, though important, group, the emergence of this group at this time must have some meaning, some explanation. We must attempt, therefore, not only to explain these views but to account for them.

Yet how does one "account for" a movement of this kind? There can be no single answer to such a question, for there can be no agreement on what constitutes a satisfactory explanation where historical causation is concerned. The psychologist will seek a psychological explanation, the sociologist a sociological one; each man will answer the question in the terms provided by his special interests. No single answer need be false, though it cannot be complete. We are seeking here for relevant truths, not for "the truth." Ideally, a complete synthesis which would yield an adequate philosophy of history might be possible, but in fact it is not possible and perhaps not desirable. The literary critic, like the historian, seeks to increase understanding of the cultural situation by elucidating relevant truths. It is for his general audience to judge of the relevance and for his fellow-specialists to judge of the truth. These are the two essential criteria. To seek for one universal truth in these fields is to risk falling short on both these criteria: it has always been a common fault in thinkers, who have a natural tendency to megalomania. In these matters the whole is not the sum of the parts, but neither is it a unity discoverable independently of the parts. There may be a point at which the series of discrete truths fuse into a unity, but it certainly cannot be predicted in advance. The whole duty of the historian of culture is to present the truths he can discover and present them with a sense of relevance. Only thus can knowledge become understanding, and "the truth" will take care of itself.

Thus, in endeavoring to account for the repudiation of the Montaigne tradition in favor of that of Pascal (as we may call the movement we have been discussing), we are seeking merely to discover some relevant truth, some correlations which throw light on the situation. Here we have a handful of men denying the perfectibility of man, the possibility of utopias, the inevitability of progress, the liberal optimism, which had been a feature—often the main feature—of Western thought for centuries. Obviously there is some failure of a tradition here, the running-down of a system. The track that men have been treading for so long has been seen to have led only into the wilderness. Eliot denies the liberal romantic tradition and writes an elaborate poem called *The Waste Land*. The relation between these two activities cannot be merely fortuitous: Eliot diagnoses the present discontents as resulting from the failure of the tradition which he consequently denies, and goes back to that other tradition, left comparatively unexplored since the Renaissance, in the hope that this will lead him out of the wilderness in which the first tradition had landed his contemporaries. Or, looking at the situation in another way, we might say that, faced with the disintegration of traditional values, Eliot undertook a retrenchment much more fundamental than that of either the Georgians or the Imagists, for while these two groups sought to stem the tide of disintegration by retiring within a narrow-walled fortress—a fortress built *inside* the larger fortress which was crumbling—Eliot abandoned the larger fortress altogether and sought refuge in an older fortification, unused for three hundred years, which he attempted to repair and refurbish. To continue the metaphor, we might say that the younger poets who came after Eliot tried to solve the problem by building a new fortress, designed especially to meet the present situation. There are thus three groups—those who met the problem by limitation of the existing tradition, those who met it by going back to an older, long-abandoned, tradition, and those who tried to create a new tradition. They were all facing the same problem, though whether they were facing it consciously is another question.

If we explain the position of Hulme and of Eliot as arising from an attempt to compensate for a failing tradition, we have still to make the further explanation of why the tradition should be failing. There is obviously some connection here between the cultural situation and the completion of the great middle-class movement which began with the crumbling of the Middle Ages and produced in its progress most of the culture of Europe between (in England) the rise of the Tudors and the death of Queen Victoria. The exhaustion—we shall say "temporary exhaustion" to avoid going beyond the existing facts—of middle-class culture, which has a frequently noted correlation with the economic situation, can be related to the breakdown of the Montaigne tradition that is observable in many forms in the first forty years of the twentieth century. It was this that sent Hulme and Eliot back to

Pascal: they had reached a blind alley and turned back to seek another road. Whether that other road had not previously been shown to have also led to a blind alley is perhaps a matter of opinion.

We must not be too literal or too dogmatic in our interpretation of the situation. When we say "the exhaustion of middle-class culture," we do not mean that because the capitalist system was beginning to decline no good literature could be produced. But we do note a decline in the spontaneity of literary production, an increase in self-consciousness among writers (which brought many desirable new techniques in its wake, but which is nevertheless a sign of exhaustion), confusion of values in both creation and criticism, the rapid growth and equally rapid decline of new "schools," the cultivation of eccentricity and types of freakishness in art, uncertainty among writers concerning the nature and extent of their audience with the resultant growth of cliques and coteries, the disappearance of accepted standards and representative critical spokesmen, complete confusion concerning the methods of recruitment to the literary profession, the disappearance of all apparatus for gauging and establishing the prestige of the artist in the community, and similar signs of the unstable basis of culture. These can surely be related to other and equally obvious signs of instability on the social and economic levels.

We have noted that the Imagists tried reformation "from within," limiting and concentrating the existing tradition. But this takes into consideration only one aspect of the Imagist movement. In another of its aspects it represented a return to the older "classical" tradition and the abandonment of the "romantic" (in Hulme's interpretation of both these terms). Of the three reactions to the contemporary problem which we have indicated above, the Imagists chose partly the first, partly the second. In so far as Hulme was an Imagist and provided the movement with a philosophy, and as Eliot was an Imagist in some of his early poems (such as "Preludes" and "Landscapes"), imagism has affinities with the general intellectual position of both these writers. But what we might call the philosophical aspects of imagism were ignored by the Imagists proper, who were concerned simply with producing hard, clear verse and avoiding sloppiness. But Eliot saw the movement as Hulme saw it, rather than as H. D. or John Gould Fletcher did, and as a result he expanded and deepened the movement until it became something very different. This is not to say that Eliot consciously set himself the task of redeeming imagism from the limitations of its orthodox adherents, but this in fact is what he achieved.

The main fault of Imagist poetry in its orthodox expression was that it was completely static. The poets had no adequate sense of form, concentrating their attention on the expressive power of the individual image rather than on the relation of these images to the poem as a whole. Their poetry lacked organic quality; it was still and painted. But Eliot, one of whose dominant qualities as a poet is his sense of form, gave Imagist poetry a dialectic. Having both a sense of form and an attitude (both conspicuously lacking in most Imagist poetry, though Aldington did not lack the latter), he was able to give his poetry a dynamic quality rarely if at all to be found among his contemporaries when he began writing. For Eliot, the image is not important merely as the concrete expression of something seen; its quality is also determined by the requirements of the poem as a whole and it combines with the other images in the poem to produce a complex and dynamic unity. For example, when H. D. writes

> The hard sand breaks,
> And the grains of it
> Are clear as wine

the image here is appreciated in isolation; we appreciate its *justness*, and our appreciation is not affected by what is said in the remainder of the poem. Sometimes her poems consist of a single stanza containing a single image, so that there can be no appeal to anything except the justness of that image. But when Eliot writes

> Let us go then, you and I,
> When the evening is spread out against the sky
> Like a patient etherised upon a table

the function of the image here is not that of simply describing a phenomenon justly; the simile has a function in terms of the mood and meaning of the poem as a whole. We cannot indeed answer the question whether the line

> Like a patient etherised upon a table

is a "just" image until we have read the complete poem, and when we have done so we realize that though Eliot might have given us many other equally accurate descriptions of the evening sky, only this particular description will do in this context; the poem *requires* an image of helplessness and disease at this point, to set the tone and the mood and to combine with other images and incidents to produce the total effect at which the poet aims. In H. D.'s poetry the appeal is wholly to the natural world; in Eliot's it is partly to the natural world but also—and more urgently—to the rest of the poem. When Eliot continues

> Let us go, through certain half-deserted streets,
> The muttering retreats
> Of restless nights in one-night cheap hotels

we realize that the use of adjectives here is motivated by something more than the desire for accurate representation. The deliberate choice of the definite yet indefinite adjective—"*certain* half-deserted streets"—combines with later suggestions of anonymity ("In the room the women come and go") and shadiness ("Streets that follow like a tedious argument/Of insidious intent") to fill out the essential meaning of the poem. The same can be said of adjectives like "muttering" and "restless": they set that note of purposeless activity which is so important in the poem's construction. And, to illustrate the difference between merely naturalistic and organic imagery, we might ask why Eliot should mention that Prufrock passes "one-night cheap hotels/And sawdust restaurants with oyster-shells" on his way to pay his visit when he undoubtedly must pass other less depressing institutions on the same journey. The answer is, of course, that Eliot picks out from an infinity of possible images (each "true" on the naturalistic level) those which will combine most effectively and most significantly with the other images and incidents in the poem. This opening stanza of "The Love Song of J. Alfred Prufrock" both initiates the plot and lays down meanings which are necessary to the subsequent development of the poem, so that these images give added meaning to future images and the future images reflect back on these images to complete the circle of meaning. This is what we mean when we say that Eliot gave imagism a dialectic. He is every bit as hard and precise in his use of images as the Imagists are, but he also gives his images an organic function which is not to be found in orthodox Imagist poetry. This could be illustrated and elaborated by an analysis of any one of Eliot's poems.

This quality of Eliot's is not, of course, unique. Most great poets use images organically. Yet it was a quality lacking in both the Georgians and the Imagists, and he restored it to modern poetry. It might be argued that Eliot was able to do this because, instead of trying to escape from attitudes (which was the way the Georgians and the Imagists tended to meet the disintegration of values), he returned to an older scheme of values to which he adhered in his work and in terms of which he could make his poetry into significant patterns. I. A. Richards got the situation completely reversed when he asserted that in *The Waste Land* Eliot effects "a complete severance between poetry and *all* beliefs"—a statement which, if it means anything, seems to mean that Eliot here was writing a poem without adopting, or showing signs of having adopted, any attitude whatever. This is true of Joyce's *Ulysses*, but it is the very reverse of the truth as far as Eliot is concerned. You only see the waste land as waste if you have something to which to compare it; you deplore heresy only if you accept an orthodoxy; you talk of damnation only if you believe in the possibility of salvation. Eliot deplored a generation without values just because he himself had values, had a standard on which to judge his generation and to find it in the waste land. Further, it is often (and surprisingly) forgotten by critics of Eliot that *The Waste Land* is not a pessimistic poem asserting that there are no values and there never can be any: the poem concludes with the thunder speaking its message of salvation (asserting values) and with the descent of the fertilizing rain. The contradiction between Eliot's earlier and later positions, which some critics profess to see, does not exist. It is true that in his earlier he concerns himself with the negative (critical) task, and in his later with the positive (propagandist) one, but you must have values before you can be critical, and Eliot's illumination of the hollowness of contemporary middle-class activity in his early poems derives from the same attitude which he expresses directly in much of his later work. There is certainly development in Eliot's intellectual position, but there is no rightabout-face—unless we are to interpret his very recent poem "East Coker" (May, 1940) as a recantation of his whole earlier position and a lapse into complete and weary skepticism.

Thus it might be argued that Eliot was able to bring dialectic into modern poetry (from which it had for some time been banished) because he also brought back into it positive belief. Whether that belief was reactionary or progressive is irrelevant to our present point: an Indian summer may herald winter, but it is nonetheless warm while it lasts. The relation between belief or attitude and structural quality in poetry is not of course direct and simple. The position is that if a writer has a stable value standard he can more confidently present poetic situations in dialectical patterns than if he has none, for if he has none his symbols can have no certain meaning and therefore their relation to each other will be obscure. It would seem also that in an age of multiple faith, where the symbols become not meaningless but ambivalent, the dialectic can become most brilliant and most subtle. By an age of multiple faith we mean not an age of universal belief but an age where the poet and his public are equally receptive to two or more different sets of beliefs—as was John Donne, for example, for whom difference did not mean mutual exclusiveness as it came to mean in times that were intellectually more settled. There comes a point at which multiple belief can scarcely be distinguished from confused belief: the metaphysical influence on the younger English poets of the 1930's, for example, can be interpreted as arising from the latters' intellectual eclecticism which has something in common with Donne's Janus-faced quality. But multiple belief itself often implies tolerance, and tolerance is often—if unconsciously—based on skepticism, as the case of Sir Thomas Browne will show, so that, paradoxically, skepticism can be the basis of multiple belief as well as of the rejection of all belief. These are difficult questions, but questions very relevant to a discussion of modern poetry, as will appear in our discussion of the poets of the 1930's.

The influence of the seventeenth-century metaphysical poets on modern poetry cannot be wholly explained by some similarity between the intellectual position of the two ages. Eliot, on whom this influence is considerable, had, it is true, great sympathy with the Anglican position of a poet like Herbert, but Eliot's Anglicanism is hardly that of the seventeenth-century poets, and in general his intellectual position is far removed from the "intellectual climate" of the seventeenth century. Eliot's point of contact with the metaphysicals was rather his desire to make poetry more cerebral, to resolve the conflict between sensation and ratiocination, between emotion and reason, between passion and logic, which lay behind so much of the poetic practice of the preceding age. We have noted how he brought a dynamic quality to the static poetry of the Imagists, how he gave it a dialectic. This can be linked up with his classicism (in Hulme's sense), his dislike of the romantic exploitation of vague personal emotion, his insistence on objectivity, order, and discipline which is so important in his poetry and his criticism. What struck Eliot most in contemporary life was its lack of order, its lack of any hierarchy of values, and his poetic career represents a search for these things. Donne, too, with his "unified sensibility" and mastery of poetic dialectic, was one who, seeing unity in diversity (and able to insist on the diversity because he could trust his fundamental integrating power to manifest itself in the *form* of his verse), made order out of chaos. To achieve order in a world of chaos was Eliot's aim.

CHAPTER VI

T. S. ELIOT

WITH the passing of the nineteenth century and the completion, in its various phases, of what the textbooks call the "romantic" contribution to English poetry, the reader of poetry in England and America was left with certain definite expectations concerning the subjects with which poetry ought to deal. These expectations, derived from the more obvious aspects of a century's poetry, were so specific and so widespread that they represented a real millstone round the neck of the original poet—the poet who wished to contribute to the culture of his time by using language creatively, freshly, vividly. Such a situation was not new—it is found periodically in the history of any culture—but, owing to the tremendous growth of the reading public in the nineteenth century, the expectations of the audience for poetry at the beginning of the twentieth century were both highly influential and highly vulgar. They represented the watered-down Tennysonian tradition as it had reached the middle-class reading public through the magazine poet. That some kind of vulgarization of culture went on in the latter part of the nineteenth century can hardly be denied, yet this was not the necessary result of its democratization. One might say, however, that the democratization of culture in a community whose practical values were increasingly commercial would necessarily imply vulgarization, the middle-class reader being culturally exploited in a way that exactly parallels the physical exploitation of the working class. The phenomenon of cultural exploitation has not yet been adequately considered, nor has its precise relation to the social situation been worked out. But of its existence there can be no doubt.[1]

The early twentieth-century reader of poetry, then, came to the reading of verse with certain fixed expectations of what he would find. He would have been satisfied had he encountered poetry as dream, poetry as passive contemplation, poetry as precise word-painting, poetry as treating in verse the poet's emotions about conventionally "poetic" subjects (which were strictly limited), poetry as moral or patriotic exhortation, poetry as popular philosophy, poetry as juggling with beautiful-sounding words. The Georgians and the Imagists instead of trying to fight these expectations tried to refine and discipline them, though in doing so the Imagists at least did a great deal to break them down altogether. But no frontal attack on them had yet been made, and until such an attack had been made there could be no cure for the exhaustion of the poetic tradition. It is not that the kinds of poetry welcomed by the average reader of poetry at this time were in themselves undesirable; but they were kinds which had been so fully explored throughout the previous century that diction was becoming standardized and thus fundamentally unpoetic and inorganic, and, fur-

[1] This point, which can only be touched upon here, the author hopes to consider in detail in a later work.

ther, in limiting poetry to these kinds the public unduly restricted the field of poetry and compelled the poet to remain in this restricted and exhausted area. It is true that there were poets in the nineteenth century who had themselves transgressed beyond the established limits. Browning had done so, both in subject matter and in technique—and it is curious to see what happened to Browning as a result. He was admired, he was even worshiped, but this very worship and admiration served the function of immobilizing him. Smothered with the adoration of elderly ladies and choked with the cotton-wool of Browning societies, he was given no chance to exert any influence: the succeeding generation saw him only through the clouds of incense sent up by his female admirers, and in the haze he looked exactly like Tennyson. Thus "Tennyson and Browning" were linked together as Victorian poets, and when the reaction against the Victorian tradition came Browning suffered with the others; his "modern" qualities (and he has a great deal in common with the poets of the 1920's) were ignored, and he was dismissed as a charlatan or a sentimentalist. This process of immobilization which was (unconsciously) applied to Browning is an interesting example of what happens to a poet who is popular in his day but popular not on account of the qualities which are most characteristic of him and differentiate him from his contemporaries. It is only fairly recently that Browning has been absorbed by the English poets as a real influence.

Eliot was the first considerable English poet of the twentieth century who deliberately flouted the public expectations concerning poetry.[2] He did not do this in any sensational way, not having the talent for shouting possessed by his friend Ezra Pound, but quietly and, at first, unobtrusively, with perhaps little awareness of what he was really doing. He was able to handle language in a new and stimulating way because he was not merely a technician—and no important movements in literature are started by mere technicians, though many try to start them—but a poet who was compelled to go behind the current poetic tradition because his general intellectual position demanded it. He was out of sympathy with the whole liberal-democratic-romantic swing of culture, and thus avoided its symbols, its attitudes, its techniques. And as that particular phase of culture was in an exhausted condition at the time when Eliot embarked seriously on his poetic career, it so happened that by being reactionary he became revolutionary. There is no real paradox here. Eliot threw out the dregs of the nineteenth century which had survived into the twentieth because he objected to the whole general direction which civilization had taken in the last two centuries and wished to get behind to an earlier tradition with which he was more in sympathy and which alone provided him with a basis for creative activity. To be creative a poet must be honest, and to be honest Eliot had to be reactionary. But to be creative is often to be revolutionary, for it implies abandoning worn-out conventions of writing,

[2] We are considering Eliot here as English rather than American, as most of his poetic career has developed in England, and he is now a naturalized British subject. Ezra Pound, who is so obviously the rebellious small-town American, preceded Eliot in his flouting of public expectations concerning poetry, though he gained general recognition after Eliot.

conventional diction, stock themes and attitudes, exhausted symbols. In this sense Eliot was revolutionary: he brought a new vitality into English poetry and exerted an influence on those who sought a new vitality for reasons diametrically opposed to his own.

In what this new vitality consisted is less easy to explain. To take lines from Eliot and place them side by side with lines from one of the Georgian poets will not tell us very much, for the characteristic feature of Eliot is the nature of his poetic logic, yet even this will indicate a certain quality in the imagery that had not been seen in English poetry for a long time:

> And indeed there will be time
> For the yellow smoke that slides along the street
> Rubbing its back upon the window-panes;
> There will be time, there will be time
> To prepare a face to meet the faces that you meet;
> There will be time to murder and create,
> And time for all the works and days of hands
> That lift and drop a question on your plate;
> Time for you and time for me,
> And time yet for a hundred indecisions,
> And for a hundred visions and revisions,
> Before the taking of a toast and tea.

Not only do these images have a quality not to be found in Georgian poetry, but the transition between the images is also handled in a quite different manner. The images are not in themselves "poetic"; that is, they have none of the standard suggestions or associations which had come to be popularly considered essential in poetry throughout the nineteenth century. The casual introduction of contraries ("there will be time to murder and create"), is prepared for by no obvious

fanfare of impressive oppositions, and the seeming casualness produces the effect of surprise which is just
what is necessary to arrest the reader's attention and
prevent him from reading the poem with a vague set of
conventional expectations. It is a simple fact that
Eliot's poetry has to be read so much more carefully
than that of the Georgians. We are not carried along
on a murmuring stream with our eyes and ears half
shut: the meanings flash and glitter and change and
shock, and we must be alert, responsive, intelligent, if
we are to follow. It might be said without unfairness to
his immediate predecessors that Eliot reintroduced intelligence to the reading of poetry. Put beside the lines
from Eliot just quoted these from De la Mare:

> When music sounds, gone is the earth I know,
> And all her lovely things even lovelier grow;
> Her flowers in vision flame, her forest trees
> Lift burdened branches, stilled with ecstasies.

This is a wholly different kind of poetry: its logic is
propositional, and the imagery is used to illustrate and
embroider the proposition. The proposition sets the
mood, which the imagery elaborates. But in Eliot's
poetry the mood determines the statement, which is
not propositional but allusive, fragmentary, symbolic:

> I grow old . . . . I grow old . . . .
> I shall wear the bottoms of my trousers rolled.
>
> Shall I part my hair behind? Do I dare to eat a peach?
> I shall wear white flannel trousers, and walk upon the beach.
> I have heard the mermaids singing, each to each.
>
> I do not think that they will sing to me.

These lines are not to be considered as a series of propo-
sitions elaborated and illustrated with appropriate

imagery. They are suggestions of symbolic situations the symbolic quality (i.e., the meaning) of which is to be fully grasped only if we read the poem sufficiently carefully to allow the images expressed here to combine with earlier and later images, to reflect back on the rest of the poem and to let the rest of the poem reflect back on them. In a transition such as

> Oh, do not ask, "What is it?"
> Let us go and make our visit.
>
> In the room the women come and go
> Talking of Michelangelo,

we are not reading the poem aright if we ask "What room is this? What has it to do with the previous question? What has Michelangelo to do with it?" The room with the women, as it appears when we consider the poem as a whole, is a symbolic situation, symbolic of that empty, middle-class, drawing-room society whose atmosphere is one of the most essential parts of the poem. The De la Mare poem we can read and appreciate with our intelligence almost lulled to sleep, but the Eliot poem demands cerebration if it is to be understood. This is what differentiates Eliot from the French Symbolists who so influenced him. The French Symbolists not only can but ought to be read with a lulled intelligence, for the effect of their poems is deliberately made to depend on suggestion only, on images sensed in that half-awake state when they are most allusive and least limited. Eliot's poetry has all the suggestiveness of the French Symbolists, but it has a much more complex kind of organization than their poetry has, and, further, the suggestiveness manifests itself only to the alert intellect. The influence of the

Symbolist poets blends with that of the seventeenth-century metaphysical poets.

The function of the prefatory motto in Eliot's poetry—often a quotation from some earlier poet—is to set the mood or tone with reference to which the symbols and images that occur within the poem proper are to be interpreted. They are not simple displays of erudition or philosophical tags, but devices employed for the purpose of elucidating the poet's terms. For example, "The Love Song of J. Alfred Prufrock" is the title (the title nearly always being an integral part of the poem with Eliot), which is known to be ironic when we read the quotation from Dante, with its note of hopelessness and emptiness,

> S'io credesse che mia riposta fosse
> A persona che mai tornasse al mondo,
> Questa fiamma staria senza piu scosse.
> Ma perciocche giammai di questo fondo
> Non torno vivo alcun, s' i' odo il vero,
> Senza tema d'infamia ti rispondo.

This quotation resolves a certain opposition contained in the title—"The Love Song of J. Alfred Prufrock," where "love song," with its romantic connotations, stands in a puzzling relation to the prosaic business-man's name "J. Alfred Prufrock": we know, after reading the quotation, that the poet's mood is one of irony and despair and that the opposing suggestions in the title between lyrical passion and the behavior of the prosaic middle-class modern conveys the emptiness of the modern situation. With the theme thus clarified we proceed to the opening stanza, where (if we read it with the preparation the poet has already given us) the images take on the necessary meanings and combine in the manner intended by Eliot. So by the end of the first stanza a new unity has been achieved (title, quotation, and the stanza itself combining into a single complex of meanings) which, in turn, both interprets and is interpreted by the succeeding stanza, and so on throughout the poem. This is the method not only of "Prufrock" but also of "Portrait of a Lady," "Rhapsody on a Windy Night," "Mr. Apollinax," and "La Figlia che piange"—all written between 1910 and 1917—as well as of most of the 1920 poems (which include "Gerontion," "Sweeney Erect," and "The Hippopotamus"). Eliot's contribution to the revitalizing of English poetry was made near the very beginning of his poetic career.

It is perhaps significant that these early poems contain most of Eliot's best work.[3] In his concern at the death-in-life which modern civilization appeared to him to be, he was led to express himself in a more cogent, a more intellectual, manner than the one current at the time when he began writing. There is of course no simple cause-and-effect relationship here, but there does seem to be a correlation between Eliot's attitude and his technique. He saw around him a society without values, an exhausted civilization, gesturing impotently in accordance with the barren formulas of a worn-out humanism. As a man, he was highly sensitive to order, pattern, hierarchy—the very qualities which appeared to him to be lacking in the contemporary situation. As a poet, he displayed these same tendencies in his interest in form, in structure, in poetic

[3] At least, up to the time of writing (June, 1940).

dialectic. He was thus in a position to make a two-fold attack on the modern world, in *what* he wrote and in *how* he wrote it. In subject matter he employed themes which implied criticism of the emptiness and flabbiness of modern life and thought, while in technique he employed every means he could to avoid that flabbiness which he was criticizing. But when, later on, he turned from criticism to preaching remedies, that double link between subject matter and technique was lost. Further, it might be argued that his criticism was conceived more earnestly than his remedies, so that in much of his later poetry we detect a loss of force. But this kind of technique requires that the poet should conceive of his subject with a high degree of passionate conviction, for otherwise the careful and precarious relation between the images will not communicate itself to the reader; there will be no incentive to him to make the effort of organization, of reference back and forth: the reader must be arrested, surprised, shocked into continual alertness if he is to carry with him as he reads the cumulative effect of Eliot's poetic logic. If Donne were simply a complacent Anglican divine, he could not have been an effective metaphysical poet (the difference in vitality between Donne and Herbert is instructive here), and similarly the quality of subdued yet desperate protest in Eliot's early work enabled him to exploit his metaphysical technique to greatest advantage, while the more quiescent—we might say acquiescent—note in so much of his later poetry tends to remove that central drive that provides the spark to ignite his poetic logic. It would be a mistake to drive this point too far, but it cannot be denied that Eliot as a poet of simple faith lacks the integrating power of the Eliot who is a voice crying in the wilderness.

Eliot's conservatism led him to revolution. His sense of the effeteness of twentieth-century liberal humanism, which constituted his response to the disintegration of traditional values which was taking place at ever increasing speed in post-Victorian England, and not only in England, impelled him to try to get in touch with a more stable past in terms of which the present might be condemned and remedied. In this lay his conservatism. He carefully fostered a sense of order, of pattern, of tradition, which he applied alike to politics, religion, and literature. This led to his being reactionary in politics, traditionalist in religion—and to some extent revolutionary in poetry. Yet his poetic technique is revolutionary only in a very special sense: in his desire to avoid sloppiness (which he considered the modern vice) he looked for a new and complex poetic discipline, which he achieved by combining the symbolic qualities of Laforgue, Rimbaud, Verlaine, and Corbière with the dialectical qualities of the Jacobean poets; and in his desire to identify himself with the past, to make his poetry part of a continuous tradition, he was led to introduce types of allusiveness, references to earlier representatives of the European and other cultural traditions, images based on multiple suggestions depending on simultaneous evocation of a great variety of earlier events in cultural history, which gave his work at once a richness and an obscurity that puzzled his first readers. In his earliest poems this tendency is indulged in with restraint and effectiveness, and such obscurity as exists is not a barrier but a challenge to the reader to keep his faculties alert. Thus the reference to Hesiod's *Works and Days* in "Prufrock"—

> There will be time to murder and create,
> And time for all the works and days of hands
> That lift and drop a question on your plate—

is not difficult to grasp, while its force is immediate; the suggestion of contrast between worth-while and worthless activity which has been made in so many different ways in previous sections of the poem ("the women come and go/Talking of Michelangelo"—the contrast between futile drawing-room conversation and the vital nature of its subject) is given a new turn, a new implication. But in *The Waste Land* and some later poems this desire to carry the past constantly with him as compensation for the hollowness of the present leads to types of allusiveness which tend to clutter up the poem rather than to light it up. It is important to realize that obscurity in Eliot is due to his too self-conscious traditionalism. Some critics complain of Eliot's pedantry; but it is not pedantry: it is the desire to bridge the gulf between an ordered past and a chaotic present with his own person.

That Eliot was self-conscious to a most unusual degree about tradition can hardly be doubted. We can see this not only in his poetic practice but also in his critical work. This self-consciousness is itself an indication that something is wrong. In a stable civilization where works of art are produced with spontaneity and without undue explanation or apology the poet does not stop to consider whether he ought to be "traditional" or not. But Eliot is constantly worrying about this question. His feeling that his age has lost contact with the past is a reflection of the cultural problem of his period—the problem of how to produce art in an age which is becoming increasingly emptied of common values, of assumptions about the nature of things shared by artist and public. Eliot pleads that a poet should have "historical sense" which, he explains, "compels a man to write not merely with his own generation in his bones, but with a feeling that the whole of the literature of Europe from Homer and within it the whole of the literature of his own country has a simultaneous existence and composes a simultaneous order."[4] Now few would deny that the greatest artists probably do have such a feeling, though it can hardly be a conscious one. But, on the other hand, few will believe that it is a feeling which can be consciously acquired. You cannot set out to acquire historical sense in Eliot's sense of the phrase. It develops organically as part of your education or it does not come at all. The Englishman will find something characteristically American in this doctrine of Eliot that a man ought to set out and acquire culture, just as he finds Ezra Pound's cultural posturings suggestive of an American women's club. Whether a man has this historical sense or not depends on the age into which he is born, not on the number of books he has read or the number of allusions to Dante he can bring into his poetry. The truth is, there seems to be something monstrously artificial about all this preoccupation with tradition that we find in Eliot. When he enunciates with

[4] "Tradition and the Individual Talent," *Selected Essays, 1917–1932* (New York, 1932), p. 4.

prophetic fervor such a principle as this: "No poet, no artist of any kind, has his complete meaning alone: his significance, his appreciation is the appreciation of his relation to the dead poets and artists," he is uttering a simple commonplace of criticism. As though any poem could be judged, or ever has been judged, "alone"! Our whole approach to literature is conditioned by its past, whether we realize this or not. But Eliot expresses this as a new principle. It is important for him that this should be emphasized, because he is stressing those things which he believes his age to lack. It argues a certain naïveté for an important poet to tell his public solemnly that the poet "must be aware that the mind of Europe—the mind of his own country—a mind which he learns in time to be much more important than his own private mind—is a mind which changes, and that this change is a development which abandons nothing *en route*, which does not superannuate either Shakespeare, or Homer, or the rock drawing of the Magdalenian draughtsman."[5] This is the sort of thing that might be explained by a schoolteacher to a class of eleven-year-olds. We find this same naïveté in Eliot's belief that a poet can demonstrate and communicate his sense of tradition, his "historical sense," by building quotations from and references to past authors into his works. We cannot help feeling that a properly developed historical sense will not demonstrate itself in this crude fashion and that Eliot's frantic desire to establish contact with the past arises largely from his discontent with the present and not from any historical sense at all. We begin to suspect that Eliot

[5] *Ibid.*, p. 6.

is compensating for his lack of an organically developed historical sense (a lack shared, perhaps, by his generation) and that he gives the game away by overcompensation. It might be added that in his stress on tradition there is also another factor at work—Eliot's protest against the romantic individualism which judged merit by uniqueness, a protest that had been eloquently voiced by Hulme, who probably influenced Eliot in this respect.

The Waste Land has been Eliot's most discussed poem, and it has given its name to a period. Though not his best poem it is in many respects his most important, for it represents his attempt to solve the cultural problem of his time. The basis of the poem is a multiple myth, deriving largely from Jessie L. Weston's book *From Ritual to Romance* and partly from other sources, such as Frazer's *Golden Bough* and the Upanishads. The myth seeks to express the barrenness and desiccation of modern civilization, the need for refreshment and new vigor which is longed for but cannot come until regeneration has been effected; with that moral regeneration the rain descends and the long drought comes to an end. Eliot is not content with expressing this theme in a simple fable form. He intertwines several fables—the story of the grail, primitive vegetation myths, the Christian story of the resurrection, and many others—each of which has the same moral. He switches from one to the other and refers to one while employing the other throughout the poem. Here is tradition with a vengeance: almost all the great myths of the world are called into service. It is thus that Eliot tries to solve the cultural problem of his time. In a poem stating that problem and its solution he endeavors to speak with the voice of the ages, with the voice of universal man, using all tongues, employing all myths, bringing the whole of the past bodily into the present. If the contemporary world has no generally accepted myth, no common background of belief to hold it together, then Eliot will write in terms of all beliefs, committing himself not to any specific one of them but to a belief in the importance of belief. For Eliot the idea of faith is always more important than any specific faith, the concept of order more important than any given order, the sense of the past more important than any one aspect of the past. So in *The Waste Land* he rolls all previous orders and beliefs into a ball and tosses it into the modern world. Has he solved the problem of being traditional in an age which lacks tradition, or has he simply demonstrated more clearly than ever the existence of the problem? Let the reader decide.

Obscurity is inevitable in a poem which depends to such a degree on allusiveness. Eliot recognizes this by appending notes ("Cf. Ezekiel II, i"; "Sylvan scene. V. Milton, *Paradise Lost*, IV, 140"; "The interior of St. Magnus Martyr is to my mind one of the finest of Wren's interiors"; "Cf. Hermann Hesse, *Blick ins Chaos*"; "Cf. *Inferno*, XXXIII, 46 . . . . also F. H. Bradley, *Appearance and Reality*, p. 346"; etc.) which constitute one of the most shocking phenomena in literature. Here is a poet cheerfully admitting that he has been unable adequately to objectify his thought in terms of his medium so that he must add what is "left over" in notes, explanations, and references at the end of the poem. There has been a great deal of special pleading concerning this device of Eliot. One critic explains:

> On the particular matter of what is accomplished by Eliot's literary allusions, and what equipment is necessary to comprehend them, consider the opening passage of "The Fire Sermon."
> . . . . If one reads these lines with an attentive ear and is sensitive to their sudden shifts in movement, the contrast between the actual Thames and the idealized vision of it during an age before it flowed through a megapolis is sharply conveyed by that movement itself, whether or not one recognizes the refrain to be from Spenser. If one does have the lovely picture of his "Prothalamion" in mind, there is then added to the contrast a fuller volume and poignancy. In like manner with the startling quickening of pace in the final two lines and the terrifying shudder they induce: it is not necessary to refer this effect to Marvell's "Coy Mistress," although if the effect of the sudden electric shift in cadence in that poem is also in the reader's ear, there is again a heightening.[6]

Are we to understand, then, that it is not necessary to know what the author is saying, because the way in which he says it gives you the idea anyway? And that if you happen to know what the author wants to say in addition, then you appreciate the poem even more? This suggests that the poet inserts. optional meanings for the cultured. But surely we cannot distinguish in this way between a minimum (vague) meaning and a maximum optional meaning. When a poet says something, he means it, and he means it all. Nor are we satisfied when we are told that "in neither of these cases is anything demanded of the reader different in kind from what is demanded by Milton's *Lycidas*." *Lycidas*, like every poem written in the seventeenth

[6] F. O. Matthiessen, *The Achievement of T. S. Eliot* (London, 1939), pp. 45–46.

century in England, drew for its imagery on biblical and classical sources, with which Milton's audience was familiar and with which the modern audience must be familiar if it wishes to understand the poem. The Bible and the classics were part of the cultural background of the time, which the poet of the period had every right to take for granted. But Eliot by including those notes at the end admits that he cannot take for granted the background which he is utilizing. When we are told further that "the point with any poem is that if the reader starts by being enchanted by the movement of the lines, then gradually his mind furnishes itself with the information necessary to understand what they are telling him,"[7] are we to understand that on reading *The Waste Land* we first allow ourselves to enjoy the line movement, and then we sit down to read Jessie Weston's book, another book entitled *The Proposed Demolition of Nineteen City Churches* (see Eliot's note on l. 264), Henry Clarke Warren's *Buddhism in Translation*, Chapman's *Handbook of Birds of Eastern North America*, Hermann Hesse's *Blick ins Chaos*, Deussen's *Sechzig Upanishads des Veda*—to all of which the reader is referred in Eliot's notes, not to mention the score of more familiar works to which reference is also made? But surely there is a fundamental difference between a poem and a bibliography. It is quite true that in reading a poem we "start by being enchanted with the movement of the lines" and then attempt a fuller understanding by more careful reading. But this fuller understanding comes from within the poem; we have to read more carefully, more sensitive-

[7] *Ibid.*, p. 47.

ly. Of course, if the book is one written in a previous age, we must familiarize ourselves with the references, which were known to the poet's public in his day but not in ours. That is a legitimate preparatory establishment of text and is something quite different from a situation where the poet asks his contemporaries to refer to works fairly obscure even in his own day.

There can be no doubt that *The Waste Land* has power and beauty and cogency in certain of its parts, yet the fact remains that the multiple myth is too complex for any reader to be able to read the poem fully at any given time and that our enjoyment is frequently spoiled by our tripping over cultural lumber that has been deliberately left lying about by the poet. It is not difficult to understand the reason for Eliot's procedure in the poem. He is addressing to a generation which lacks a tradition an indictment of that generation—one item in the indictment being precisely that the generation does lack a tradition—and he overcompensates for that lack by employing an eclectic cultural background self-consciously and, as it were, chastisingly. For all its brilliant handling of language and its use of that poetic logic which we have already discussed, *The Waste Land* is rather an important document in the history of culture than a perfectly executed poem. Critics, tending to confuse its historical importance with its intrinsic merit, apply confused criteria and find the poem "great." In a sense it is great, but we must be careful to define that sense.

"The Hollow Men," one of the simplest and most effective of Eliot's poems, presents no such problem. Carefully organized, brilliantly phrased, the poem is an

impressive symbolic picture of an age without belief,
without value, without meaning:

> We are the hollow men
> We are the stuffed men
> Leaning together
> Headpiece filled with straw. Alas!
> Our dried voices, when
> We whisper together
> Are quiet and meaningless
> As wind in dry grass
> Or rats' feet over broken glass
> In our dry cellar.

The precision and cogency with which Eliot uses images here ("hollow"—there is nothing of their own
within; "stuffed"—all within is borrowed, artificial;
"leaning together"—they have no independent voli-
tion, they go in herds; etc.) show how effectively he
utilized the legacy of the Imagists; but there is more
than precision of imagery here, there is extreme sub-
tlety and effectiveness of organization as the poem
moves from the bleating chorus to the individual nightmare and on to the picture of the cactus land, the hopeless waiting for death, and the final whimpering conclusion. This is the death-wish of an age without hope,
because without belief. Eliot always considered it more
important to have a strong belief, even if it were wrong,
than to have a weak belief or none at all. Above all, it
must be an objective belief, not the promptings of the
individual "inner voice," on which he poured such
scorn. A "coherent system of dogma and morals" is
convenient even if it is not true, and it is not a far step
from this position, which Eliot maintains in his essay
on Dante, to the position that maintains that belief

matters more than truth. It is significant that Eliot asks "What is *right?*" and not "What is *true?*"[8] What Eliot seeks is authority and order, anything rather than the mushy individualism which he held responsible for the contemporary disintegration. He believed that it is better to go to Hell than to Limbo, better to be positively evil than neither good nor evil. The fault of the hollow men is not that they are villainous; it is that they are not even villainous; they are empty, neither good nor evil. The Waste Land is a land without values, where one cannot even commit a crime, for there is no standard on which it could be judged a crime. When Eliot turned to the Anglican church, many were surprised, but it was not a surprising step.

Most of Eliot's subsequent poetry has struck a note of quiet Anglican hope, though occasionally the old critical note is struck with vigor. "Ash Wednesday," with its winding logic, runs the gamut of despair and hope to come to rest in peaceful acquiescence. "Marina" has that limpid quality that develops in Eliot's later poetry. And then there are his verse plays where with a new simplicity Eliot has sought a new audience. But it is no part of the present study to catalogue Eliot's works or expound them in detail: this task has been adequately performed by other critics. This much might be said of Eliot's later work: he has been busy seeking new myths that will express his Christian faith to a wider audience than that which he addressed in his early poetry. He has lost some of his early vigor and some of that sense of play which expressed itself even in his grimmest poems, but he retains his gift of phrase

[8] *Selected Essays*, p. 17.

and his organizing ability. As a force in English poetry he is spent; his contribution has been absorbed by younger poets, to whom he has nothing more to give. As the disintegration which first challenged Eliot proceeded apace he clung more and more to the traditional order which he had accepted in joining the Anglican church. His literary criticism became more theological, and an ecclesiastical glow spread over his work. His preoccupation with tradition had finally landed him squarely in the past, and the younger English poets, whose eyes were earnestly scanning the future, came to regard him with that respect which is generally reserved for the great dead.

CHAPTER VII

W. B. YEATS—I

Eliot's concern with tradition, his attempt to define his relation to the past, his attack on the romantic view of literature as the exploitation of personality, and his deliberate eclecticism in his choice of symbols from past cultures suggest some of the problems of the poet who lives in an age without a stable background. Self-consciousness about symbols and about tradition—and symbols depend upon tradition —is to be found increasingly among European poets from the last decade of the nineteenth century onward. Probably no poet was so aware of this problem and made such a gallant and sustained effort to solve it as W. B. Yeats. Yeats's poetic career, beginning in the 1880's and concluding in the latter part of the 1930's, coincides with the development of that disintegration of belief which had so great an influence both on the technique and on the subject matter of literature. The phases of his poetic activity represent successive attempts to compensate for this disintegration by framing for himself symbolizations of experience in terms of which he could give meaning to his symbols, pattern to his thought, coherence to his interpretation of experience. Though he shared his problem with his generation, he differed from most of his contemporaries in being more conscious and deliberate in his endeavor to solve it. In his earliest period he saw the

problem as that of finding a substitute for a no longer
tenable religious tradition:

> I am very religious, and deprived by Huxley and Tyndall,
> whom I detested, of the simple-minded religion of my childhood,
> I had made a new religion, almost an infallible church of poetic'
> tradition, of a fardel of stories, and of personages, and of emo-
> tions, inseparable from their first expression, passed on from gener-
> ation to generation by poets and painters with some help from
> philosophers and theologians. I wished for a world, where I could
> discover this tradition perpetually, and not in pictures and in
> poems only, but in tiles round the chimney-piece and in hangings
> that kept out the draft.[1]

In his search for a compensating tradition Yeats
went first to romantic literature, and then to mysticism
of one kind and another, to folklore, theosophy, spiritualism, Neo-Platonism, and finally elaborated a symbolic system of his own, based on a variety of sources,
and in terms of this was able to give pattern and coherence to the expression of his thought. It was a
search for a system rather than a search for a set of
beliefs; he sought a mode of expression rather than a
set of dogmas to express. The problem for Yeats was
not that of finding what he ought to say: his sensitive
and restless mind provided him with a constant supply
of subjects and attitudes. His problem was that of giving order and proportion to his insights. He did not
even seek a point of view, for his mind, so much more
elastic and all-embracing than Eliot's, would never be
satisfied, as Eliot's was, with any single formulation of
attitude. He sought simply adequacy of poetic communication and for that he needed an ordered system
to give meaning to his terms, significance to his symbols, form to his expression, and unity to his individual

[1] *Autobiography of William Butler Yeats* (1938), p. 101.

poems. He did not conceive of this system as demanding the intellectual assent of his readers, though his attempts at prose exposition show that he would have preferred such assent: its function was to be rather that of the frame on which the weaver weaves his patterns, necessary to the weaver though requiring no recognition on the part of those who appreciate the finished product. The analogy is not altogether perfect, for in some cases we do need to know what frame Yeats was using before we can appreciate his finished work. Indeed, there seems to be some confusion in Yeats's conception of the function of his system. Is it a frame for the weaver or a key to be used by the observer in interpreting the pattern aright? In a period of cultural stability such a system would serve both functions, but it would be a system common to writer and reader and it would serve these functions unconsciously. In the modern world, however, the poet who wishes to compensate for the lack of such a tradition has to make up his mind how far the compensation should go. For by attempting too much he may achieve nothing, by trying both to help himself to coherence and to supply a background of belief for his readers he may end by making himself incoherent or by alienating his readers by the privateness of his conceptions. This is a risk which Yeats often runs in his later poetry, and though he often emerges successfully by his power of organization and the brilliance of his phrasing (the first communicating the relation of the symbols to each other, the second evoking sufficient suggestion of their meaning to combine with the suggestion of their relation to each other and produce a significant whole), there are occasions, in some of the poems in "Words for Music Perhaps," for example, where the reader gets only the impression of an esoteric imagination. Did not Yeats possess this double power of organization and of phrasing, his work would be more consistently obscure than in fact it is.

It is a mistake to consider Yeats as a mystical poet. The true mystic is one who seeks to escape from an age of overformulation by repudiating the orthodox categories and seeking identities and correspondences not recognized by more rational speculation. But far from seeking to escape from formulas Yeats is seeking to establish them. He does not wish to escape from orthodox religion but to find a substitute for it. He seeks to impose order, not, as the true mystic does, to break down a too neatly ordered system and get beyond it. He has little in common with a mystical poet like Æ. He turns to mysticism not in search of shattering new insights but in quest of categories, often maintaining a casual skepticism concerning what to the mystics themselves were the essential truths. His discussion of Macgregor Mathers, for example, in *The Trembling of the Veil*, is conducted in an almost ironical spirit; the real point was that "I had soon mastered Mathers' symbolic system," and a new way of ordering experience had been discovered. Like Eliot, Yeats was looking for order. But while Eliot was able to find it in orthodox Christianity, for Yeats, as for so many of his contemporaries, "Victorian science" destroyed the possibility of belief in orthodox Christianity, and he had to turn to less beaten tracks. That Victorian science had also, by implication at least, destroyed the possibility of belief in these other systems did not matter, for Yeats had as a very young man believed in the scientific approach and allowed it to destroy his religious belief which could never after that be re-established, while he came to these other systems after he had repudiated Victorian science (which he soon grew to hate "with a monkish hate") which could thus have no further effect on his attitude. It might be argued that the question of belief was in any case irrelevant, for it was a vague sort of quasi-belief that Yeats came to have in these systems, and why could he not have adopted this same attitude to religion? The answer to this is simply that the religious tradition was too finally blown up for Yeats in his youth for him to be able to turn there for his system. It has often been noted that in an age when religious belief is decaying, belief in all kinds of odd superstitions grows apace: astrology flourishes more vigorously in England today than it did when Christianity was more firmly in the saddle. The truth is that when a religious tradition begins to decay those who are affected by its decay are rarely conscious of any logical process of repudiation which could be applied a fortiori to the superstitions which often take its place; they simply have a vague sense that the tradition has decayed, the position is untenable, relating this feeling, perhaps, to the name of some scientist, as Yeats did to the names of Huxley and Tyndall, which came to take on a symbolic meaning for him.

System, order, ritual—these Yeats sought not for their own sake, not because as a man he would have chosen to subordinate his mind and body to a traditional discipline, but because he needed them as a poet, to help him achieve adequate poetic expression. Again and again in his autobiographical writings we find some such wish expressed:

I planned a mystical Order which should buy or hire the castle, and keep it as a place where its members could retire for a while for contemplation, and where we might establish mysteries like those of Eleusis and Samothrace; and for ten years to come my most impassioned thought was a vain attempt to find philosophy and to create ritual for that Order. I had an unshakable conviction, arising how or whence I cannot tell, that invisible gates would open as they did for Blake, as they opened for Swedenborg, as they opened for Boehme, and that this philosophy would find its manuals of devotion in all imaginative literature, and set before Irishmen for special manual an Irish literature which, though made by many minds, would seem the work of a single mind, and turn our places of beauty or legendary association into holy symbols. I did not think this philosophy would be altogether pagan, for it was plain that its symbols must be selected from all those things that had moved men most during many, mainly Christian, centuries.[2]

Here Yeats is expressing his desire for an eclectic symbolic system which would at once be a source of literary symbolism and derive from the symbolism of imaginative Irish literature. The reference to Ireland in this connection is interesting; for we cannot hope to understand Yeats if we do not realize that his search for a symbolic system was bound up in a very complex manner with his desire to utilize traditional Irish material— literary, historical, mythical, and popular. In some way Ireland had to be involved in his system; Irish symbols had to be employed to give the proper emotional quality to his work. Yeats was attempting to solve two problems—the general problem of symbols in literature in an age lacking a common tradition and

[2] *Ibid.*, pp. 217–18.

the particular problem presented by the confusions of the Irish situation. We have only to go through Yeats's autobiographical writings to see at once that the chaotic nature of the Irish scene—politically, culturally, socially—imposed a task on him from the beginning, the task of imposing order on this chaos. It was, of course, a subjective order primarily, a pattern in his own mind which would enable him to utilize Irish material in his poetry. He was no politician and did not feel called upon to solve the practical problems of his time. But he was impelled to find a way of putting Ireland into some mental order, so that cultural symbols of dependable significance would be at the disposal of the artist. This double task—one posed by the cultural problem of his time, the other resulting from his relation to Ireland—was faced boldly by Yeats, and his development as a poet is the record of how he attempted to carry it out.

When Yeats first began writing poetry, he accepted as a matter of course the thinned-out romantic tradition which demanded that poetry should be concerned with a "beautiful" world of dream, employing a language chosen for its vague emotional suggestiveness and conventional poetic associations. He had at this period no clear ideas concerning his relation to his Irish background; the influences on him were English rather than Irish, and in his treatment of Irish themes he displayed the normal English romantic attitude toward things Celtic. But even in this earliest period his thin poetizing seems to have meant more to Yeats than the conventional practice of a craft; the images of beauty and strangeness which he collected out of

Spenser and Shelley and other less distinguished influences were intended in some vague way to represent
an imaginative world of values which would compensate him both for his lost religion and for the confused
and prosaic nature of everyday existence. He was already seeking his "infallible church of poetic tradition." But he had as yet no thought of a system; his
church was to be built on the romantic word, compensating for the grayness of contemporary reality:

> The woods of Arcady are dead,
> And over is their antique joy;
> Of old the world on dreaming fed;
> Grey Truth is now her painted toy;
> Yet still she turns her restless head:
> But O, sick children of the world,
> Of all the many changing things
> In dreary dancing past us whirled,
> To the cracked tune that Chronos sings,
> Words along are certain good.

There are poems on Indian subjects, too, among this
early group, India being chosen for its remoteness and
its romantic suggestions in accordance with a tradition
established by generations of English poets. At this
time—he was not yet twenty—Yeats held the belief that
"only beautiful things should be painted, and that only
ancient things and the stuff of dreams were beautiful."[3]
His poetry was frankly escapist, like most early verse of
nineteenth-century poets, and its purpose was not to
interpret life but to compensate for it. Spenser, Shelley, Rossetti, and Blake shaped his adolescence, and he
struck Byronic poses to his reflection in shop windows.
It was Ireland that rescued him from this imitative

[3] *Ibid.*, p. 73.

romanticism. In the folklore that he picked up while staying with his grandparents in Sligo he found a subject matter as effective for his purposes as India or Arcadia and much less hackneyed, while in the peasant speech of the Irish country people he found a diction and a rhythm which, while poetic, was fresh and vigorous. We have only to compare "The Stolen Child" or "To an Isle in the Water" with "The Indian to His Love" or "Anashuya and Vijaya" to see what the introduction of the Irish folk element meant for Yeats's poetry. There is a new precision of imagery and a greater vitality in diction in the former poems, whose theme and setting are Irish, introducing the imagination of the Irish peasants and the places—Rosses, Sleuth Wood, Sligo—that he knew. The substitution for vague romantic landscapes of specific Irish scenes associated with local folklore of a kind that combined wild imagination with homely realism—stories of fairies, ghosts, goblins, local spirits—was the first important step in the development of Yeats's individuality as a poet.

This change worked slowly in Yeats's poetry, and its full effect was not immediately noticeable. It would be quite wrong to think of Yeats as suddenly turning to realistic poetry while still in his teens. The general nature of his poetry remained the same, but the imagery became more precise, the setting more clearly seen and so more clearly presented, the themes less pretentious. *The Wanderings of Usheen* (later spelled by Yeats *The Wanderings of Oisin*), written in his early twenties, still shows very clearly his early influences—Spenser and Shelley and the Pre-Raphaelites—and in its general trappings and looseness of structure displays Yeats's most youthful characteristics. Yet this elaborate narrative poem, based on an Irish mythological theme, contains passages of sharp and disciplined writing that stand out from the prevailing luxuriance as heralds of the later Yeats.

But it was not simply Irish folklore and peasant speech that influenced Yeats's poetry at this time. A more important impetus came from his Irish background. Yeats has explained it himself:

I think it was a Young Ireland Society that set my mind running on "popular poetry." We used to discuss everything that was known to us about Ireland, and especially Irish literature and Irish history. We had no Gaelic, but paid great honour to the Irish poets who wrote in English, and quoted them in our speeches. . . . . I knew in my heart that most of them wrote badly, and yet such romance clung about them, such a desire for Irish poetry was in all our minds, that I kept on saying, not only to others but to myself, that most of them wrote well, or all but well. I had read Shelley and Spenser and had tried to mix their styles together in a pastoral play which I have not come to dislike much [*The Island of Statues*], and yet I do not think Shelley or Spenser ever moved me as did these poets. I thought one day— I can remember the very day when I thought it—"If somebody could make a style which would not be an English style and yet would be musical and full of colour, many others would catch fire from him, and we would have a really great school of ballad poetry in Ireland. If these poets, who have never ceased to fill the newspapers and the ballad-books with their verses, had a good tradition they would write beautifully and move everybody as they move me." Then a little later on I thought, "If they had something else to write about besides political opinions, if more of them would write about the beliefs of the people like Allingham, or about old legends like Ferguson, they would find it easier to get a style." Then, with a deliberateness that still surprises me, for in my heart of hearts I have never been quite certain that one should be more than an artist, I set to work to find a style and things to write about that the ballad writers might be the better.[4]

Yeats is beginning to be conscious of his search for a tradition and at the same time to use Ireland to help him in his search.

By this time the "Irish revival" had got under way, and Yeats did not have to depend entirely on his own eye and ear in utilizing Irish motives in his poetry. Already in 1878 Standish O'Grady had published his *History of Ireland, Heroic Period*, a florid and high-spirited work which, whatever its faults as a piece of scholarship, was of tremendous importance in making available to the public the old Gaelic heroic legends. Wrote Yeats:

> In his unfinished *History of Ireland* [O'Grady] had made the old Irish heroes, Fion, and Oisin, and Cuchullan, alive again, taking them, for I think he knew no Gaelic, from the dry pages of O'Curry and his school, and condensing and arranging, as he thought Homer would have arranged and condensed. Lady Gregory has told the same tales . . . . but O'Grady was the first, and we had read him in our teens.[5]

While O'Grady's history thus made available material from the heroic age of Irish history, the popular legends and folk literature of Ireland were collected and edited soon after, providing even richer subject matter for the poets. George Sigerson's *Poets and Poetry of Munster* began this task as early as 1860, and it was followed by the same author's *Bards of the Gael and Gall* in 1897, which contained about a hundred and fifty traditional

---

[4] "What Is 'Popular Poetry'?" *Ideas of Good and Evil (Collected Works in Verse and Prose of William Butler Yeats*, Vol. VI [Stratford-on-Avon, 1908]), pp. 2–3.

[5] *Autobiography*, pp. 189–90.

Irish poems translated in a meter which endeavored to capture the movement of the Gaelic originals. Douglas Hyde's *Love Songs of Connacht* (1893) was even more influential; the Gaelic poems were translated by Hyde into "that dialect which gets from Gaelic its syntax and keeps its still partly Tudor vocabulary," and Yeats profited greatly.

> Nothing in that language of his was abstract, nothing worn-out; he need not, as must the writer of some language exhausted by modern civilization, reject word after word, cadence after cadence; he had escaped our perpetual, painful, purification. . . . . When I first read it, I was fresh from my struggle with Victorian rhetoric. I began to test my poetical inventions by translating them into like speech.[6]

Yeats has several times testified to the importance for him of Hyde's *Love Songs of Connacht* and "that English idiom of the Irish-thinking people of the West."

But in London Yeats's poetic milieu was the Rhymers' Club, "which for some years was to meet every night in an upper room with a sanded floor in an ancient eating-house in the Strand called The Cheshire Cheese." Here he met with Lionel Johnson, Ernest Dowson, Richard Le Gallienne, T. W. Rolleston, John Todhunter, John Davidson, and others. Of these "companions of The Cheshire Cheese" only Rolleston and Todhunter had any association with the Irish movement, and the latter's was brief. Though there was little agreement on poetic ideals among the group, the prevailing aim was that of a rather tired sensationalism, and Yeats was not very sure whether to dissociate himself from it or not. The influence of the French Symbolists reinforced that of the Pre-

[6] *Ibid.*, pp. 375–76.

Raphaelites, and gradually "the reds and yellows that Shelley gathered in Italy" faded out of his poetry to give place to less violent colors. His Irish material, too, encouraged him in this tendency, but on the whole the lessons he was learning from Ireland and those he was learning from the "decadent" poets in London hardly fitted together, and, as is clear from his autobiographical writings, Yeats remained in a rather confused state of mind throughout the late 1880's and early 1890's.

Among Irish sources he continued his search of new myths and a living speech that could be used in poetry, and he did so less as a patriot than as a poet. He had as yet no literary plans for Ireland or for himself in Ireland; he was waiting for something, though he was not quite clear what it was. He was in fact waiting for some kind of opportunity to integrate the disparate elements of a poetic creed that he had picked up in Ireland and in London. It became increasingly clear to him that only in Ireland, only by defining his relation to Ireland and putting the symbols of Ireland in order in his mind, could he achieve the kind of poetic system he was groping after. In 1890 he wrote, significantly: "We are preparing, likely enough, for a new Irish literary movement—like that of '48—that will show itself in the first lull in politics." As long as the Irish revival remained primarily a political movement Yeats at this stage could derive little from it as a movement, and give little to it; but with a "lull in politics" he might be able to make Ireland serve his purpose.

The death of Parnell, following rapidly on the virtual collapse of his movement, provided that lull for which Yeats was waiting. There came to him "the sudden certainty that Ireland was to be like soft wax for years to come," and he bestirred himself to insure that he should be the one to mold that wax to a shape that would serve both literature and himself. He founded the Irish Literary Society in London and the National Literary Society in Dublin and began to conceive of himself as taking part in a movement. He came into intimate contact with the most important leaders of Irish thought of the day, whose portraits he draws in "Ireland after Parnell" (*The Trembling of the Veil*, Book II). But his practical schemes did not come to anything; he argued and quarreled and became increasingly aware of his isolation. And this was not because he was essentially an impractical person who was bound to bungle things of this sort—some years later while working for the Abbey Theatre with Lady Gregory he achieved a great deal—but because he was out in search of a mythology, a tradition, a system to help him in writing poetry, while his colleagues were interested in more objective aims. Until he had patterned his thought to his own satisfaction he could be of little use to even literary movements; his procedure was to plunge into them, engage in a short spell of great activity during which he had a great many ideas and talked a great deal, and then retire with his booty, as it were. What he was seeking is perhaps indicated by the fact that during this same activity he was also frequenting "a house in Ely Place, where a number of young men lived together, and, for want of a better name, were called Theosophists."[7] Here lived artists, Neo-Platonists, hypnotists, vegetarians, mystics of sev-

[7] *Ibid.*, p. 203.

eral varieties, a motley group of unorthodox thinkers (Æ. was the "saint and genius" of the community) whose discussions Yeats attended. It was at this time that he had the conviction that the invisible gates would open for him as they opened for Blake and imaginative literature would become the storehouse of the symbols of the new philosophy.

The Neo-Platonic ideas which he picked up at Ely Place and from Spenser and Shelley were used by Yeats at this time to give meaning and pattern to the Irish heroic themes which were coming more and more into his poetry. *The Rose* (1893) is a collection of poems whose general theme is the symbolization of Platonic "ideas" by means of figures from Irish mythology and early history. The Platonism of Shelley and Spenser is clearly seen in his conception of the Rose as a symbol of the idea of beauty, though in a note to these poems written in 1925 Yeats comments: "I notice upon reading these poems for the first time for several years that the quality symbolized as The Rose differs from the Intellectual Beauty of Shelley and of Spenser in that I have imagined it as suffering with man and not as something pursued and seen from afar." The relation of the Rose to the Irish figures is indicated in the opening poem of the group:

> Red rose, proud Rose, sad Rose of all my days!
> Come near me, while I sing the ancient ways:
> Cuchulain battling with the bitter tide;
> The Druid, grey, wood-nurtured, quiet-eyed,
> Who cast round Fergus dreams, and ruin untold;
> And thine own sadness, whereof stars, grown old
> In dancing silver-sandalled on the sea,
> Sing in their high and lonely melody.

> Come near, that no more blinded by man's fate,
> I find under the boughs of love and hate,
> In all poor foolish things that live a day,
> Eternal beauty wandering on her way.

And the concluding lines are significant:

> Come near; I would, before my time to go,
> Sing of old Eire and the ancient ways:
> Red Rose, proud Rose, sad Rose of all my days.

Ireland, especially the Ireland of heroic legend, is welcomed as his new subject, to be interpreted through his Neo-Platonic system. The influence of O'Grady's *History* is to be seen here again and again, but it is an influence absorbed and utilized for Yeats's own purpose. With the increased confidence afforded him by the mental pattern that underlies these poems Yeats was able to achieve a new power of phrase and effectiveness of structure. "The Rose of the World," perhaps the most perfect of his early poems, shows a careful discipline in language and control over form that are to be the outstanding features of Yeats's later poetry. The luxuriance and the romantic beating about the bush of his very first poems, when he sought his system in words merely ("Words alone are certain good") have given place to an artistic restraint which carries much greater power:

> Who dreamed that beauty passes like a dream?
> For these red lips, with all their mournful pride,
> Mournful that no new wonder may betide,
> Troy passed away in one high funeral gleam,
> And Usna's children died.

The use of classical and Irish names as illustration and climax to the Neo-Platonic theme, the handling of the line-lengths, the skilful placing of the emphatic words, and the simple yet effective tripartite structure of the complete poem show that this temporary synthesis of Yeats's ideas (he was to move on to many others) helped him to mature as a poet.

It was not only Irish heroic motives which Yeats managed to treat in this symbolic manner in the poems of *The Rose;* folk themes are also employed in the same manner. "The Man Who Dreamed of Faeryland," one of the most interesting and most successful of the poems using folk themes, treats popular beliefs and superstitions in a highly symbolic way, so that the story of a man involuntarily in touch with supernatural forces emerges from a catalogue of wonders:

> He stood among a crowd at Drumahair;
> His heart hung all upon a silken dress,
> And he had known at last some tenderness,
> Before earth took him to her stony care;
> But when a man poured fish into a pile,
> It seemed they raised their little silver heads,
> And sang what gold morning or evening sheds
> Upon a woven world-forgotten isle
> Where people love beside the ravelled seas;
> That Time can never mar a lover's vows
> Under that woven changeless roof of boughs:
> The singing shook him out of his new ease.

The contrasts wind through the subsequent stanzas, becoming at once more complicated and more clear, until the climax, where the man's restless and unwanted desire for supernatural truth reaches its culmination: he is dead and would have slept in peace

> Did not the worms that spired about his bones
> Proclaim with that unwearied, reedy cry
> That God has laid His fingers on the sky,

That from those fingers glittering summer runs
Upon the dancer by the dreamless wave.
Why should those lovers that no lovers miss
Dream, until God burn Nature with a kiss?
The man has found no comfort in the grave.

We see here what is to become Yeats's characteristic
ability to create a myth whose meaning lies in its form,
its pattern, rather than in its precise connotation. The
connotations of such a myth as that expressed in "The
Man Who Dreamed of Faeryland" are numerous, perhaps infinite, and this is true of a great deal of Yeats's
later poetry and plays. He was concerned with truth as
pattern rather than with truth as a "state of affairs."

This feature of his poetry can once again be related
to that conscious desire to create a system, to build a
body of tradition in terms of which his symbols would
have significance, which we have noted as one of the
central facts about Yeats's development as a poet. We
note in these early poems a general tendency to construct a pattern in terms of a simple pair of contrasts.
Human activity as opposed to fairy activity, the natural
as opposed to the artificial, the familiar as opposed to
the remote and strange, the domestic as opposed to the
heroic, the contemporary as opposed to the ancient,
the transient as opposed to the permanent—these contrasts provide nearly all the themes in *Crossways* and
The Rose. Yeats's awareness of a dichotomy in human
experience was central in his thought; his earlier attitudes are concerned largely with expressing this dichotomy, while in his later work we see him endeavoring to
resolve it. But always it is the pattern that matters.
The terms in which this division is expressed vary from

poem to poem, but the fact of the division is constant. And so in his later work—*The Tower* and *The Winding Stair*—where he constructs elaborate symbols and strange myths in order to achieve a resolution of this contrast, it is the resolution rather than the terms of the resolution that matters. If we understand this important aspect of Yeats's thought, we shall find his later poetry less obscure and his mythology less irritating.

About the same time that he was writing the poems contained in *The Rose* group, Yeats was collecting and recording in simple prose the folk material from which he drew his symbols in the poems. These records are contained in the group of prose sketches which he called *The Celtic Twilight;* they include descriptions of his favorite spots—of Drumcliff and Rosses, for example—accounts of local superstitions, and all sorts of folk tales and folk beliefs. To some extent this collection represents the raw material out of which the poems were constructed. Yet they are not simply that; Yeats intended to achieve in this simple recording the same task that he sought to achieve in his poetry. He tells us in his Introduction:

> I have desired, like every artist, to create a little world out of the beautiful, pleasant, and significant things of this marred and clumsy world, and to show in a vision something of the face of Ireland to any of my own people who would look where I bid them. I have therefore written down accurately and candidly much that I have heard and seen, and, except by way of commentary, nothing that I have merely imagined.[8]

Here again is the desire for order, for pattern, with Irish material used as a means of achieving it.

Though Yeats's participation in Irish affairs at this

[8] *The Celtic Twilight* (*Collected Works*, Vol. V), p. 1.

time, his foundation of the literary societies, and his utilization of Irish material arose from his desire to satisfy his personal need as a poet, he nevertheless believed that in thus making use of Irish material he was contributing as much to Ireland as the politicians and the fighters. The concluding poem of *The Rose*, "To Ireland in the Coming Times," makes this point quite clearly:

> Know, that I would accounted be
> True brother of a company
> That sang, to sweeten Ireland's wrong,
> Ballad and story, rann and song;
> Nor be I any less of them,
> Because the red-rose-bordered hem
> Of her, whose history began
> Before God made the angelic clan,
> Trails all about the written page.

And he goes on to claim kinship with the more political of the Irish writers:

> Nor may I less be counted one
> With Davis, Mangan, Ferguson,
> Because, to him who ponders well,
> My rhymes more than their rhyming tell
> Of things discovered in the deep,
> Where only body's laid asleep.

We have here his expression of the relation between his philosophic and his patriotic interests.

In *The Wind among the Reeds* (1899) the influence of the French Symbolists—of Mallarmé, of Verlaine, of Villiers de l'Isle Adam, and also of Maeterlinck—is more clearly seen than anywhere else in Yeats's work, but it is still Irish figures and Irish themes that supply the bulk of his symbols. He had been reading the mystical writers, too, Böhme and Swedenborg, and studying Blake for the edition of Blake's prophetic books which he undertook along with Edwin Ellis. His prose works *The Secret Rose* and *The Tables of the Law* present the result of the various mystical speculations in which he had been engaged in the 1890's, while some of the essays in *Ideas of Good and Evil* express the view of poetry which he came to hold as a result. His symbolic system became more élaborate and tied up more definitely with specific figures in Irish mythology and Irish heroic history. Yet the precise significance of these symbolic figures—Hanrahan, Michael Robartes, Aedh, and others—is not always clear; they are used to give pattern and general implication rather than precise denotation to the poems, as is indicated by the fact that Yeats dropped these names from his later revisions of the poems, substituting simply the pronoun "he." Thus the title "Michael Robartes Remembers Forgotten Beauty" becomes in the revision "He Remembers Forgotten Beauty" and similarly "Aedh Mourns for the Loss of Love" is altered to "The Lover Mourns for the Loss of Love." This change is an important clue to the function of Yeats's symbolic systems, indicating that they were intended to help himself more than the reader, so that once he had completed the poem the framework could later be removed without loss. Once again we see Yeats's search for order and system, to be imposed on a world without tradition.

Yet the views on symbolism which Yeats had by this time come to hold showed certain confusions, in particular the confusion between mysticism and magic which is one of the qualities that distinguish him from the true mystic. His discussion of magic in *Ideas of Good*

W. B. YEATS

and Evil (1901) illustrates his state of mind on these matters:

> I find in my diary of magical events for 1899 that I awoke at 3 A.M. out of a nightmare, and imagined one symbol to prevent its recurrence, and imagined another, a simple geometrical form, which calls up dreams of luxuriant vegetable life, that I might have pleasant dreams. . . . . I find another record, though made some time after the event, of having imagined over the head of a person, who was a little of a seer, a combined symbol of elemental air and elemental water. This person, who did not know what symbol I was using, saw a pigeon flying with a lobster in his bill. I find that on December 13, 1898, I used a certain star-shaped symbol with a seeress. . . . . She saw a rough stone house, and in the middle of the house the skull of a horse. . . . . I know that my examples will awaken in all who have not seen the like, or who are not on other grounds inclined towards my arguments, a most natural incredulity. It was long before I myself would admit an inherent power in symbols. . . . . I cannot now think symbols less than the greatest of all powers whether they are used consciously by the masters of magic, or half unconsciously by their successors, the poet, the musician and the artist. . . . . The symbols are of all kinds, for everything in heaven or earth has its association, momentous or trivial, in the great memory, and one never knows what forgotten events may have plunged it, like the toadstool and the ragweed, into the great passions.

And he concludes the essay with this appeal:

> Who can keep always to the little pathway between speech and silence, where one meets none but discreet revelations? And surely, at whatever risk, we must cry out that imagination is always seeking to remake the world according to the impulses and the patterns in that great Mind, and that great Memory?[9]

He puts the matter concisely at the beginning of the same essay:

> . . . . I believe in three doctrines, which have, as I think, been handed down from early times, and been the foundations of nearly all magical practices. These doctrines are—

[9] *Ideas of Good and Evil (Collected Works,* Vol. VI), pp. 47 ff.

(1) That the borders of our minds are ever shifting, and that many minds can flow into one another, as it were, and create or reveal a single mind, a single energy.

(2) That the borders of our memories are as shifting, and that our memories are a part of one great memory, the memory of Nature herself.

(3) That this great mind and great memory can be evoked by symbols.[10]

Yeats clarifies his view further in his essays on "Symbolism in Painting" and "The Symbolism of Poetry" (the first written in 1898, the second in 1900). In the former essay he quotes with approval a German Symbolist who insisted that "Symbolism said things which could not be said so perfectly in any other way, and needed but a right instinct for its understanding; while Allegory said things which could be said as well, or better, in another way, and needed a right knowledge for its understanding."[11] This distinction between symbolism and allegory clarifies some aspects of Yeats's art: it explains his casualness in providing (or not providing) his readers with keys to the esoteric systems on which so much of his symbolic poetry and drama is based. If the symbols fell into the right order and had the right relation to each other, the reader with "a right instinct" would grasp their significance. Precise knowledge was unnecessary.

The importance of arrangement is stressed by Yeats himself more than once, for example in discussing the well-known lines of Burns—

> The white moon is setting beyond the white wave,
> And Time is setting with me, O!

[10] *Ibid.*, p. 23. [11] *Ibid.*, p. 177.

These lines Yeats calls "perfectly symbolical" and explains: "Take from them the whiteness of the moon and of the wave, whose relation to the setting of Time is too subtle for the intellect, and you take from them their beauty. But, when all are together, moon and wave and whiteness and setting Time and the last melancholy cry, they evoke an emotion which cannot be evoked by any other arrangement of colours and sounds and forms."[12] According to Yeats, the indefinable yet precise emotions possessed by "all sounds, all colours, all forms" arise either from their "pre-ordained energies" or from "long association." He is not careful to distinguish these sources in practice, and indeed the two are often confused. The emotional value of the names of the old Irish heroes, for example, arises from the nature of the stories in which they figure, from the part they have played in history, mythology, and in previous literature, and no theory of "pre-ordained energies" is necessary to explain it. Yet Yeats seemed at one time to believe that each of these names possessed such a preordained energy, which could be depended on to communicate itself to the reader. However, his theory never quite controlled his practice, and his use of place names and the names of Irish figures in *The Wind among the Reeds* suggests no consistent reliance on these energies.

The poetry of *The Wind among the Reeds* contains some of the most effective of the tenuous symbolic poetry that Yeats wrote. He left behind now for good the lush romantic descriptions of his earliest period, while at the same time the tapestry quality of so many of the

[12] *Ibid.*, pp. 188–89.

poems of *The Rose* has given place to a more fluid kind of verse. This change is not unrelated to the development in Yeats's attitude—his elaboration of a symbolic system and of a theory of symbolism—as he explains himself:

> If people were to accept the theory that poetry moves us because of its symbolism, what change should one look for in the manner of our poetry? A return to the way of our fathers, a casting out of descriptions of nature for the sake of nature, of the moral law for the sake of the moral law, a casting out of all anecdotes and of that brooding over scientific opinion that so often extinguished the central flame in Tennyson, and of that vehemence that would make us do or not do certain things. . . . . With this change of substance, this return to imagination, this understanding that the laws of art, which are the hidden laws of the world, can alone bind the imagination, would come a change of style, and we would cast out of serious poetry those energetic rhythms, as of a man running . . . . and we would seek out those wavering, meditative, organic rhythms, which are the embodiment of the imagination, that neither desires nor hates, because it has done with time, and only wishes to gaze upon some reality, some beauty.[13]

It might be argued that in all his critical and expository work Yeats was moved by a desire for over-rationalization, that he was seeking to find a rational explanation of ways of writing which he had already come to practice intuitively. There is some truth in this; we find in Yeats constantly the order-seeking intellect glossing and expounding and rationalizing texts which might have more meaning if left to speak for themselves. But this does not mean that we should be justified in ignoring his prose work when discussing his poetry, for his prose does show more explicitly than his poetry the lines along which his mind was moving at

13 *Ibid.*, pp. 198–99.

the time and thus provides valuable help in an endeavor to explain and interpret his changing attitudes and the relation of these changes to his poetic practice. The eccentricity—and on occasions the plain silliness—of Yeats's thought is sometimes taken as an example of an innate confusion of mind, but the very opposite is the truth. It was his nostalgia for order and system in a world whose orthodox systems had ceased to be able to provide them that led Yeats into these esoteric paths. Of course, there were other reasons too: the fact that he began to develop as a poet in the 1880's and 1890's left a permanent legacy to his poetry that one is tempted to dismiss too lightly in view of the extreme individuality of Yeats's later achievement. But the fact remains that Yeats became an esoteric symbolist for the same reason that Eliot became an Anglican and W. H. Auden a Socialist: each was seeking a solution to the problem presented by a disintegrating tradition.

We find in the poems of *The Wind among the Reeds* the same deep sense of contrast which we have already noted in Yeats's earlier poetry. The Christian is opposed to the pagan, the normal to the supernatural, the passing to the changeless. The opening poem, "The Hosting of the Sidhe," describes the gathering of the fairy folk with a tremendous sense of their difference from humanity and a careful exploitation of proper names:

> The host is riding from Knocknarea
> And over the grave of Clooth-na-Bare;
> Caoilte tossing his burning hair,
> And Niamh calling *Away, come away:*
> *Empty your heart of its mortal dream.*

In "The Everlasting Voices" we have the contrast between life in time and life outside time, round which the poem is constructed: a similar contrast between the fairy and the human (related to the contrast between the pagan heroic and the Christian) is the basis of "The Unappeasable Host"; while the contrast between the world of human morality and the changeless values of "the mystical brotherhood/Of sun and moon and hollow and wood" is the theme of "Into the Twilight." These are random examples, but they illustrate a feature of Yeats's poetic structure which is one of the most central facts about his art. He continually uses his symbols to express a sense of difference, not of identity, and he does this in innumerable forms, until finally, in his later verse, he finds in the symbol of the winding stair the key to a new attitude and a new kind of expression. This is a point to be stressed, for our interpretation of Yeats's later poetry depends on it.

But the folk strain was still running through Yeats's poetry, curbing his esoteric impulses and producing every now and again a simple, realistic poem which foreshadows what some critics have called the "realistic period" that comes in the middle of his poetic career. "The Song of the Old Mother," for example, is a short, simple, realistic poem describing the hard domestic life of an Irish peasant woman. Theories of symbolism seem to have been forgotten, and all Yeats is doing is etching a picture he remembers having seen. It was fortunate for Yeats that he kept his photographic eye; it was one of the anchors that kept him tied to earth even in his wildest and most fantastic speculations. The recurring ballads and simple descriptive poems in his work show that he never surrendered himself to any single theory of what poetry ought to be.

With *The Wind among the Reeds* what one might call Yeats's first period comes to a close. It is of course silly and unrealistic to draw hard and fast lines between the different phases of a poet's development; all one can say is that from his earliest work to this collection Yeats is working in some modification of the "romantic" tradition of the late nineteenth century, with the influence of Shelley, Blake, and the Pre-Raphaelites clearly noticeable in his poetry. He was not yet clearly distinguishable from any of the other poets of the period who were concerned with beauty, antiquity, and the exploitation of a meditative romantic imagination. With *In the Seven Woods* (1904) we see clearly the transition not only to a new style—that had been seen already—but also to a new poetic ideal. In *The Green Helmet and Other Poems* (1910) that transition is completed and the first great metamorphosis of Yeats is achieved. What that change was and what it meant is worth some inquiry.

CHAPTER VIII

W. B. YEATS—II

LOOKING back in 1906 on the work of his earliest period Yeats found that he had mistaken the poetic ideal:

Without knowing it, I had come to care for nothing but impersonal beauty. I had set out on life with the thought of putting my very self into poetry, and had understood this as a representation of my own visions and an attempt. to cut away the nonessential, but as I imagined the visions outside myself my imagination became full of decorative landscape and of still life. I thought of myself as something unmoving and silent living in the middle of my own mind and body. . . . . Then one day I understood quite suddenly, as the way is,· that I was seeking something unchanging and unmixed and always outside myself, a Stone or an Elixir that was always out of reach, and that I myself was the fleeting thing that held out its hand. The more I tried to make my art deliberately beautiful, the more did I follow the opposite of myself. . . . . Presently I found that I entered into myself and pictured myself and not some essence when I was not seeking beauty at all, but merely to lighten the mind of some burden of love or bitterness thrown upon it by the events of life. We are only permitted to desire life, and all the rest should be our complaints or our praise of that exacting mistress who can awake our lips into song with her kisses. . . . . We should ascend out of common interests, the thoughts of the newspapers, of the marketplace, of men of science, but only so far as we can carry the normal, passionate, reasoning self, the personality as a whole.[1]

The abandonment of "impersonal beauty," the desire to "carry the normal, passionate, reasoning self"

[1] *The Cutting of an Agate* (London, 1912), pp. 68–70.

into his poetry, is seen in the poems of *In the Seven Woods* and *The Green Helmet*. He no longer endeavors simply to embroider patterns out of old myths, to present symbolic situations; the true patterns of life are to be found instead in the poet's interpretation of his own experiences. This is not to say that Yeats abandons any of his attempts to evolve a universal system, but rather that he comes to believe that an impressive poetry can be more adequately attained by interpreting in terms of his system experiences that have been significant for him. He had, of course, written poetry in the first person earlier, though his very earliest poetry is almost entirely dramatic in the sense that the poet is not speaking in his own person but in that of conventional romantic figures. The question with which Yeats is concerned at this time is not the conventional one of the difference between lyrical and dramatic poetry. It is the twofold problem of how to make his poetry whole and how to make it dynamic. To solve this problem Yeats repudiated the view that there is an inevitable distinction between the poet as a man, as a "doing and suffering" human being, and the poet as a creator of "beauty." The poet as creator gives form to his experiences as man, and his poetry acquires impressiveness and completeness as a result of dignity of style; the poet must be aristocratic in his attitudes and his expression—it is this that removes him from the market place—and if he attains "style, mastery, that dignity and that lofty and severe quality Verlaine spoke of," he is then able to produce whole and vital poetry even when "lightening the mind of some burden of love or bitterness thrown upon it by the events of life." There

is a shift of emphasis from content to form, partly because Yeats seems to have felt that his earlier tapestry
poetry had lacked vitality and had not succeeded in
patterning experience in the way he sought to do, and
partly because, becoming as he was more and more
involved with the confusions of the contemporary Irish
situation, he felt more and more the need to express his
own reactions to this situation and thus sought a more
autobiographical type of poetry. He no longer lives in
Ireland's heroic past:

> I have forgot awhile
> Tara uprooted, and new commonness
> Upon the throne and crying about the streets
> And hanging its paper flowers from post to post,
> Because it is alone of all things happy.
> I am contented, for I know that Quiet
> Wanders laughing and eating her wild heart
> Among pigeons and bees. . . . .

He seeks to interpret his own experiences in a dignified
and polished style. We see in the poems of *In the Seven
Woods* the beginning of that epigrammatic manner
which Yeats was to bring to perfection in *The Green
Helmet*. A conscious and careful craftsmanship accom-
panies more realistic (i.e., personal and contemporary)
themes.

Thus Yeats's verse becomes more severe and "classical" in manner while his themes become more personal
and original. The older themes are not abandoned,
but the newer ones keep intruding. Thus side by side
with "Red Hanrahan's Song about Ireland," a poem
in Yeats's earlier style reminiscent of the more conventional products of the Irish revival, we find "Adam's

Curse," a closely knit poem written in an almost col-
loquial diction and dealing with a personal experience:

> We sat together at one summer's end
> That beautiful mild woman, your close friend,
> And you and I, and talked of poetry.
> I said, 'A line will take us hours maybe;
> Yet if it does not seem a moment's thought,
> Our stitching and unstitching has been naught.
>
> Better go down upon your marrow-bones
> And scrub a kitchen pavement, or break stones
> Like an old pauper, in all kinds of weather. . . . .'

Or we find the dry epigrammatic quality of "The Old
Men Admiring Themselves in the Water":

> I heard the old, old men say,
> 'Everything alters,
> And one by one we drop away.'
> They had hands like claws, and their knees
> Were twisted like the old thorn-trees
> By the waters. . . . .

We note the same tautness of style and rather weary
air of disillusion in the sad little poem, "Sweetheart,
Do Not Love Too Long," and in the plangent confession of "Never Give All the Heart."

This note of disillusion arises partly, perhaps, from
an unhappy love affair (that "miserable love affair"
which he briefly mentions in *Dramatis Personae*) and
partly from the frustration which attended so much of
his activity in Irish literary politics. He had hoped to
mold Ireland to fit the mental patterns of his poetic
system, but found that Ireland was not the soft wax under his hand that he had anticipated. He was also ir-
ritated by the pettiness and the meanness of the ordinary citizen with whom his work in Ireland brought

him into constant contact. There is a bitterness in his poetry now that is far removed from the plaintive melancholy of his earlier work.

His association with the theater also helped to change his mood. It was Lady Gregory who turned his interest in poetic drama into an active interest in the theater. She encouraged him, too, in his collection of folklore and helped to turn Yeats's interest in spiritualism among the Irish peasants into a more fruitful interest in "the dialect of the cottages"—the language that Synge used so successfully in dramatic dialogue. Lady Gregory had another important influence on Yeats; it was to some extent as a result of his visits to her home, "Coole House," that he developed his view of aristocracy in living which helped to shape his later thought and attitude and which is so important in his middle and late poetry. Yet at the same time he seemed to be accepting, though reluctantly, a view of the necessity of working with the people. "In a battle like Ireland's," he wrote to Lady Gregory, "which is one of poverty against wealth, we must prove our sincerity by making ourselves unpopular to wealth. We must accept the baptism of the gutter."[2] He began to feel a strong hatred for the Dublin middle classes who "fumble in a greasy till and add the halfpence to the pence," and was for a brief time undecided whether to ally himself with the gutter or the palace in opposition. He chose the latter, yet in no literal sense: he set before himself an ideal of aristocracy and dignity in living ("we work to add dignity to Ireland," was a favorite phrase of Lady Gregory's) which had no very clear

[2] *Dramatis Personae* (New York, 1936), p. 30.

practical implications. This ideal was but another re-flection of Yeats's desire for system, order, tradition.

All this is seen in *The Green Helmet and Other Poems*, where we note the completion of Yeats's first meta-morphosis. He is no longer living in a land of dream; he is in waking Ireland, and, though he admits now that he can find pattern and system in dealing with the world of everyday reality, he bitterly resents having to make the admission:

> Through all the lying days of my youth
> I swayed my leaves and flowers in the sun;
> Now I may wither into the truth.

Having abandoned incantatory poetry and tapestry verse, he is writing of everyday themes in a colloquial idiom with a recurring ironical note. In the opening poem he pictures himself in his earlier period "swaying upon the gaudy stern the but-end of a steering-oar" while the crowd on the shore see him as "the figure in a shroud upon a gaudy bed" and hail him by the name of Death. And he has to accept their verdict—that his earlier poetry is the poetry of the dead, not of the liv-ing, world. Is the situation simply that Yeats has found his earlier romantic and Platonic mythologizing in-capable of arousing even poetic belief, thus sending him elsewhere in his search for a symbolization of ex-perience? It would seem so, for Yeats does not remain long as a disillusioned realistic poet. Antaeus-like, he comes to earth for refreshment and inspiration; but though he retains to the end of his poetic career the col-loquial strain which this brought him—its organic rhythms, its forthrightness, its conversational quality of diction—it is not long before he introduces into his poetry new devices for symbolizing experience, new systems, and new myths.

But in the meantime his changing views and his immersion in practical work for the Abbey Theatre were encouraging him to pose as the exhausted genius, with his creative energy used up:

> The fascination of what's difficult
> Has dried the sap out of my veins, and rent
> Spontaneous joy and natural content
> Out of my heart. . . . .

His bitterness forces him to epigram, and we have short classical verses of disillusion or abuse such as "The Coming of Wisdom with Time" and "To a Poet Who Would Have Me Praise Certain Bad Poets." He contrasts with the contemporary world of petty action his ideal of aristocratic dignity, as in the poem "Upon a House Shaken by the Land Agitation":

> How should the world be luckier if this house,
> Where passion and precision have been one
> Time out of mind, became too ruinous
> To breed the lidless eye that loves the sun . . . .
> . . . . Although
> Mean roof-trees were the sturdier for its fall,
> How should their luck run high enough to reach
> The gifts that govern men, and after these
> To gradual Time's last gift, a written speech
> Wrought of high laughter, loveliness and ease?

This defense of aristocracy is difficult to reconcile with his statement to Lady Gregory that "we must accept the baptism of the gutter." But we must realize that Yeats passed through a period of confusion regarding his relation to the Irish people before eventually evolving this aristocratic ideal which he used to set against the utilitarian ideal of the middle classes. The native aristocracy of the peasant and the acquired aristocracy of the landed gentry—both depending on some kind of tradition—were both set against the activity of the shopkeeper, who had no tradition and thought only of commercial gain. In his search for a system and a tradition he could get no possible help from that very class which was responsible for the shattering of the old traditions which he was trying to replace, and this perhaps was the real reason why he turned upon it with such bitterness.

Responsibilities (1914) develops the themes and techniques that were found in *The Green Helmet*. The very title is indicative of the changed Yeats, of his later view that by accepting his responsibilities as a man he can best organize his material as a poet. He opens this collection with an apologia addressed to his dead "companions of the Cheshire Cheese." This poem, written partly in that familiar strain which is coming to be so frequent in Yeats's poetry at this time, and partly in his older mythological manner, presents a curious combination of illustrative myth and autobiographical realism which we find again and again in the later volumes—in such poems as "In Memory of Major Robert Gregory," "Broken Dreams," "A Prayer for My Daughter," "The Tower," and many others. It is this mythologizing of personal experience that marks the transformation of the simple "occasional" poetry that he was writing immediately after the abandonment of his earlier tapestry verse into a kind of poetry whose aim is once again the patterning of reality in terms of a deliberately conceived system. The apologia to his

dead friends takes the form of an invocation followed
by a fable of which the moral is that though his themes
and his manner are no longer those of Lionel Johnson
and Ernest Dowson, he is nevertheless continuing the
quest that they began, he has kept faith with his art,
and he has not betrayed his poetic integrity for transient political ends:

> I have kept my faith, though faith was tried,
> To that rock-born, rock-wandering foot,
> And the world's altered since you died,
> And I am in no good repute
> With the loud host before the sea,
> That think sword-strokes were better meant
> Than lover's music—let that be,
> So that the wandering foot's content.

The poem is written is octosyllables, a meter much
favored by Yeats at this time, partly because of its
effectiveness in epigram, partly because of its conversational suggestions. Indeed, there is much of Yeats's
poetry in this and in the succeeding collection that
reminds us of the *vers de société* of early eighteenth-
century poets like Matthew Prior; it has the same verse
movement and the same familiar strain. From Shelley
and Rossetti to Matthew Prior is a far cry, and he
seems to have made the journey by way of Walter
Savage Landor.

The anti-bourgeois note is struck continually in *Responsibilities:*

> What need you, being come to sense,
> But fumble in a greasy till
> And add the halfpence to the pence
> And prayer to shivering prayer, untill
> You have dried the marrow from the bone;

> For men were born to pray and save:
> Romantic Ireland's dead and gone,
> It's with O'Leary in the grave.

Here we see once again that simple opposition between two elements which we have noted as the basis of so many of his earlier poems. The opposition between the heroic and the commonplace has become that between the aristocratic and the commercial, the latter element in each case representing life based on no tradition and the former representing a properly patterned life. The finest expression of this contrast is to be found in that magnificent poem "To a Shade," where Yeats is addressing the spirit of a dead Irish patriot (is it Parnell?), advising him that he is better off where he is—in the grave—than in contemporary Ireland. The stately movement of the verse, the monumental phrasing, and the undulating movement of the poem, which comes to a temporary climax at the end of each of the first two verses and then to its overwhelming final climax at the end of the third and last stanza, show Yeats at his most impressive. He displays, too, the "metaphysical" quality of being able to take up more than one attitude at a time (in this case both an elegiac and an ironic one) as the third line shows:

> If you have revisited the town, thin Shade,
> Whether to look upon your monument
> (I wonder if the builder has been paid) . . . .

The emotion rises steadily to the conclusion. The first stanza ends:

> Let these content you and be gone again;
> For they are at their old tricks yet.

The contemptuous note of the indefinite "they" marks but the first step in the mood of the poem, which progresses from contempt to epic anger. The second stanza, referring to the persecution of Synge, begins mildly and rises at the conclusion to stronger abuse than the conclusion of the first:

> Your enemy, an old foul mouth, had set
> The pack upon him.

The third stanza gathers up the implications of the previous two and rises to complete the indictment of contemporary Dublin by suggesting that the Shade is safer in the tomb than among these people:

> Go, unquiet wanderer,
> And gather the Glasnevin coverlet
> About your head till the dust stops your ear,
> The time for you to taste of that salt breath
> And listen at the corners has not come;
> You had enough of sorrow before death—
> Away, away! You are safer in the tomb.

Responsibilities is a very mixed bag. Side by side with poems like those to which reference has been made, we get purely visionary poems like "The Magi," an esoteric fable that requires an explanation in the notes, and "The Cold Heaven," the record of a dream which Yeats understands symbolically, and simple symbolic poems such as "The Mountain Tomb." Yet the main tendency—toward a greater realism and familiarity, though always with a symbolic pattern in the background—is clear, and is expressed by Yeats himself in the concluding poem, "A Coat," where he tells how he made his song a coat covered with embroideries out of old mythologies, but it was imitated and worn by fools—

> Song, let them take it,
> For there's more enterprise
> In walking naked.

That Yeats was looking either below or above the middle classes for support in his search for a tradition is suggested by the poems themselves and confirmed in a very interesting manner in a note which accompanied the original edition of *Responsibilities.* Yeats wrote:

> In Ireland I am constantly reminded of that fable of the futility of all discipline that is not of the whole being. Religious Ireland—and the pious Protestants of my childhood were signal examples—thinks of divine things as a round of duties separated from life and not as an element that may be discovered in all circumstance and emotion, while political Ireland sees the good citizen but as a man who holds to certain opinions and not as a man of good will. Against all this we have but a few educated men and the remnants of an old traditional culture among the poor. Both were stronger forty years ago, before the rise of our new middle class which made its first public display during the nine years of the Parnellite split, showing how base at moments of excitement are minds without culture.

A great deal of Yeats's poetry is a commentary on this text.

It is perhaps misleading to talk of the phases of Yeats's poetic career as though they succeeded and replaced each other: the truth is that, except for his very earliest period, Yeats never left anything behind, never repudiated an earlier position, but carried the past with him into the future in a way reminiscent of the "winding-stair" technique he uses in his later poems.

He was constantly seeking a richer pattern, a more complex system, a more elaborate tradition, and he imposed his new patterns upon the old, integrating them into a richer unity, using myth and reminiscence as a means of carrying his youth into his old age. To live was, for Yeats, to "climb up the narrow winding stair to bed," and this image, so recurrent in his later poetry, is instructive. For the winding stair is both progressive and repetitious; at each landing one is above the same spot that one stood on at the lower landing, one is conscious of identity with one's lower self and yet of difference. The spiral staircase is a unity, with a definite pattern and a definite end—unlike the infinite straight line, and Yeats's progress is not in a straight line—the top of the spiral being a point which includes all the other positions in itself. The poetry of reminiscence that we find in *The Wild Swans at Coole*, *Michael Robartes and the Dancer*, *The Tower*, and *The Winding Stair* shows Yeats mentally ascending a winding stair, corkscrewing his way from the past to the present, from youth to age, advancing yet repeating, changing yet preserving, including earlier patterns in the present one. In an age without a tradition he has to build one out of his own life, making each phase of his life a chapter of a myth, and of the same myth.

With *The Wild Swans at Coole* (1919) Yeats's poetry is clearly becoming more "metaphysical" in the sense that his attitudes are more complex and ambivalent while at the same time the intellectual element in his verse becomes more important. Yet the older mythologizing continues—indeed, new myths and new systems are developed—and what we might call the metaphysical use of myth, as in "The Phases of the Moon," becomes increasingly common. A passage like the following shows an intellectual play deriving from a handling on several different levels at once of a thought-pattern which is in turn based on an esoteric myth:

> Were not our beds far off I'd ring the bell,
> Stand under the rough roof-timbers of the hall
> Beside the castle door, where all is stark
> Austerity, a place set out for wisdom
> That he will never find; I'd play a part;
> He would never know me after all these years
> But take me for some drunken country man;
> I'd stand and mutter there until he caught
> 'Hunchback and saint and fool,' and that they came
> Under the last three crescents of the moon,
> And then I'd stagger out. He'd crack his wits
> Day after day, yet never find the meaning.

The characters who figure in these poems—Michael Robartes and Owen Aherne—are figures in a complicated myth, a myth which we must understand if we are to grasp the full implication of the patterns of the poems. In a note to these poems written in 1922 Yeats informs us:

> I now consider that I used the actual names of two friends, and that one of these friends, Michael Robartes, has but lately returned from Mesopotamia where he has partly found and partly thought out much philosophy. I consider that Aherne and Robartes, men to whose namesakes I had attributed a turbulent life or death, have quarrelled with me. They take their place in a phantasmagoria in which I endeavour to explain my philosophy of life and death. To some extent I wrote these poems as a text for exposition.

This is an interesting admission and shows a development in Yeats's mythopoeic tendencies which has doubtful results for his poetry. For while his poetry was an exposition of a text (i.e., a pattern based on an implicit myth) an understanding of the text from external sources was not necessary for an appreciation of the poems; the validity of the pattern communicated itself; but when his poetry comes to be a text for exposition, and the exposition is not provided anyway, there arises a kind of obscurity which can only be penetrated by the constant application while reading of information derived from external sources. This is a distinction which most readers have sensed in Yeats's work but which few critics have admitted.

The key to much of Yeats's later symbols is to be found in *A Vision*, where he explains, for example, his view of the phases of the moon, which accounts for each phase as corresponding to a period in the history of civilization and also to a type of human character. In connection with this we have an exposition of the relation betwen a man's self and his anti-self, between a man's Will and his Mask. In interpreting human history and human character, Yeats postulates a development arising out of the opposition of antitheses and builds up an elaborate myth to illustrate his position, a myth whose dominant symbol is the "gyre," the spiral—the spinning top, the winding stair, the whirling dancer—which we meet so often in his later poetry. We have already noted something of the significance of this symbol, but its importance in Yeats's later poetry demands that we give it some further consideration.

It is of course possible to explain the winding-stair symbolism in Yeats solely in terms of the esoteric system which he expounds in *A Vision;* this has been done by more than one critic, with great skill if with doubtful profit. For if this symbolism is to have any real significance in his poetry, it must be intelligible in more general terms, it must convey a meaning to the reader who studies with care the form and pattern of the later poems without continually glossing the text as he reads. If it is not thus intelligible, the poem is to some extent a failure. That some of Yeats's poetry does fail in this way—as a result of the confusion between mythology as framework and mythology as key to the meaning of the finished work, which we have already discussed—can hardly be denied by the honest critic. The number of critics who have acclaimed the greatness of some of Yeats's later poems without giving any indication that they saw how the poems were to be construed, what the pattern was, what, to put it crudely, the poems *meant*, is an indication of the justness of a complaint voiced by Louis Macneice in a review of Yeats's *Last Poems and Plays*. "There were reviewers," wrote Macneice, "who felt Yeats was a safe bet—safe because he was an exotic; anyone can praise a bird of paradise but you have to have some knowledge before you go buying Rhode Island Reds. There is a double point that needs making—first that Yeats was not so exotic as is popularly assumed, second that on the whole his exoticism was not an asset but a liability."[3] His exoticism was not an asset when it resulted in that confusion between what helps the poet to write and what helps the reader to read which we occasionally see in the later Yeats, particularly in some of his later plays.

But some of the dominant motives in Yeats's later symbolism can be interpreted without the aid of elabo-

[3] *New Republic*, June 24, 1940.

rate prose expositions—indeed, the winding-stair image can be given more significance if we do not attempt to narrow it down to the precise intellectual meaning demanded by the system expounded by Yeats in *A Vision*. One might make a useful distinction, in reading poetry, between interpretation by exclusion and interpretation by inclusion. The former restricts its concern to the conscious intellectual ideas held by the poet, and by doing so often sacrifices richness to precision and leaves the heart of the poem invisible, while the latter seeks to extend the implications of the images by seeing all their possible relations to each other and to the poet's work as a whole. In this way we can see the winding stair as at once the symbol of progress combined with repetition, a mark of the transition from youth to old age, an illumination of the place of memory, of reminiscence, in Yeats's endeavor to see his life as a unity, and even—to put it at its most grandiose— as a theory of epistemology. The truth is to be found by the patterning of opposites until they flow into each other in a single point. But the tower with its winding staircase is ruined at the top ("I climb to the tower-top and lean upon broken stone") so that as a man grows old the past cannot be carried forward into a single point that includes both past and present, for by the time he has reached that stage his faculties are decaying; the summit of the spiral is not a point but a ruin. One could play with this idea in a hundred different ways, and each would give some sort of insight into Yeats's mind. The balancing and unifying of opposites—truth being not a state of affairs but a mental activity—can be related to Yeats's view of life as a dance, as constant movement, both progress and repetition, in the midst of which the dancer is inseparable from the dance:

> O chestnut tree, great rooted blossomer,
> Are you the leaf, the blossom or the bole?
> O body swayed to music, O brightening glance,
> How can we know the dancer from the dance?

The situation in which we cannot tell the dancer from the dance is the top of the tower, the end of the spiral, where all opposites are fused. It is by this kind of symbolism that Yeats attempts to escape the dualism which meets us in all his earlier work; the pattern, the system, is not complete so long as the opposites remain opposites, eternally divided and opposed. Yeats's quest for order is concluded only when he finds a means of completing the pattern by fusing all life into a unity: though in ascending the winding stair we go continually in different directions and keep facing and opposing our former selves, when we reach the top we are at all points on the circle's radius at the same time. Further, in looking back we see our former selves, as it were, on the empty landings, and our progress is measured as much by our increased absence below as by our increased presence above. Here we have another symbol of the unification of opposites, presence and absence being interpreted in terms of each other. Thus the presence of these spiral images in Yeats's poetry can be related to the poet's advancing age and the problems which this brings, while the fact that poetry of reminiscence becomes so common in his work at this time bears out our interpretation very nicely. For as you carry the past with you into the future, the increase in the number of your absences, in the number of places where you no longer are, is a measure of your progress; the more memories you have the older you are; and this leads us straight back to the winding stair again.[4]

But we have gone beyond *The Wild Swans at Coole*, which marks only the beginning of the spiral imagery we have just been discussing; it is in *Michael Robartes and the Dancer* (1921), *The Tower* (1928), and *The Winding Stair* (1933) that we see most clearly the tendencies that are noted above. There are other tendencies observable in the poetry of *The Wild Swans at Coole* which deserve notice before we return to the later poems. We note an increase of freedom in the handling of rhythms combined with a growing originality and variety in stanza forms. The opening poem of the group shows both these features:

> The trees are in their autumn beauty,
> The woodland paths are dry,
> Under the October twilight the water
> Mirrors a still sky;
> Upon the brimming water among the stones
> Are nine-and-fifty swans.

We see in this poem, as in so many others written by Yeats at this time and later, the thought molding the stanza pattern in the first verse and that pattern setting the model for the succeeding stanzas: thus in the first stanza, pattern depends on thought, whereas in those that follow the thought is disciplined to fit the pattern that has been worked out in the initial verse. This is just the procedure that we find followed in so many of

[4] I must here render an acknowledgment to Mr. Kenneth Burke, for some of these thoughts on the winding-stair imagery of Yeats were suggested by a poem of his which he once recited to me after we had been talking about Yeats's poetry.

the poems of John Donne, the poems opening with an outburst of passionate thought which carves its own channel and the rest of each poem keeping to the form thus carved out. But it is not only here that we find Donne's influence; we have already noted the "metaphysical" trend in Yeats's poetry at this time, and there can be no doubt that he was greatly influenced by the revival of interest in the seventeenth-century English poets which was stimulated (though not begun) by Grierson's edition of Donne in 1912. He himself lays his finger on the chief influences on him at this time:

> I know what wages beauty gives,
> How hard a life her servant lives,
> Yet praise the winters gone:
> There is not a fool can call me friend,
> And I may dine at journey's end
> With Landor and with Donne.

The self-dramatization of the poet as an old and tired man produces a great many poems at this time, and it can be easily related to some of the other motives of his later work which we have already discussed. This final system toward which he is moving, the unified pattern that he is trying to make out of his life, demands an abstract intellectual quality which he sees as a sign of old age. In the lively emotions of youth, life is full of clashing contrasts and the young man is not impelled to attempt their resolution in a cold intellectual system. But that is the only task left for the old:

> I bade, because the wick and oil are spent
> And frozen are the channels of the blood,
> My discontented heart to draw content
> From beauty that is cast out of a mould
> In bronze. . . . .

The final contrast to be resolved is that between youth and age:

> O heart, we are old;
> The living beauty is for younger men:
> We cannot pay its tribute of wild tears.

Again and again this theme is repeated:

> I have not lost desire
> But the heart that I had;
> I thought 'twould burn my body
> Laid on the death-bed,
> *For who could have foretold*
> *That the heart grows old?*

These poems are drafts for the later "Byzantium" poems, which treat the same theme more elaborately.

In his poetry of reminiscence—often constructed in long irregular verse-paragraphs, which he handles with great skill—he draws more and more on family memories and traditions; we see Yeats once again trying to relate his past to his present, this time through a common tradition that links him with his ancestors. The Pollexfens—Alfred, William, and George—stalk through his verse adding family pride as a unifying emotion.

Michael Robartes and the Dancer develops the same themes, though there is one new subject that emerges here, a subject that adds the necessary touch of passion to Yeats's new metaphysical style, so that it immediately takes wings. This is the Easter Rebellion of 1916, which inspired "Easter, 1916," and other poems. Again he treats this theme in such a way as to draw out of it a contrast between past and present and a suggestion for the resolution of that contrast:

> I have met them at close of day
> Coming with vivid faces
> From counter or desk among grey
> Eighteenth-century houses.
> I have passed with a nod of the head
> Or polite meaningless words . . . .
> Being certain that they and I
> But lived where motley is worn:
> All changed, changed utterly:
> A terrible beauty is born.

And still the problem of age and youth, of passion and intellect, of the natural and the artificial, haunts him:

> Yet am I certain as can be
> That every natural victory
> Belongs to beast or demon,
> That never yet had freeman
> Right mastery of natural things,
> And that mere growing old, that brings
> Chilled blood, this sweetness brought;
> Yet have no dearer thought
> Than that I may find out a way
> To make it linger half a day.

He consoles himself with the thought that the old man, free from the wild and clamorous calls of youth, can retire to the world of abstract intellect and perfect his system there. Yet the journey to Byzantium, though in a sense triumphant, is nevertheless reluctant.

It was not only the problems of his own old age that concerned him at this time; the age of civilization also took up his attention. We need not worry ourselves too much over the symbolic philosophy of history that Yeats evolved for himself, in terms of which he sees modern civilization as moving toward the final phase of the second subcycle, for the main point that he has to make, that in this phase of civilization

> Things fall apart; the centre cannot hold,

is equally intelligible in more conventional terms. It is the old theme: the traditions that held civilization together are decaying, and as a result pattern is giving way to chaos, things are falling apart, their relations to each other becoming more and more obscure. For the re-establishment of pattern and unity we must await the emergence of the imminent new civilization—

> Surely some revelation is at hand;
> Surely the Second Coming is at hand.

"The dream of my early manhood, that a modern nation can return to Unity of Culture, is false; though it may be we can achieve it for some small circle of men and women, and there leave it till the moon brings round its century."[5] Yeats was one of that "small circle of men and women" who tried to find a patterned unity for himself though he knew it was not possible to his generation as a whole. "A conviction that the world was now but a bundle of fragments possessed me without ceasing," he wrote of himself between 1887 and 1891, and he continued:

> I delighted in every age where poet and artist confined themselves gladly to some inherited subject-matter known to the whole people, for I thought that in man and race alike there is something called "Unity of Being." . . . . Doubtless because fragments broke into even smaller fragments we saw one another in the light of a bitter comedy, and in the arts, where now one technical element reigned and now another, generation hated generation, and accomplished beauty was snatched away when it had most engaged our affections.[6]

[5] *Autobiography of William Butler Yeats* (New York, 1938), p. 250.
[6] *Ibid.*, pp. 166–68.

This early statement of his problem can be put beside some of his later poems to show that Yeats's central ideas did not change as much as some critics think; what did change was the systems he evolved in order to express those ideas.

In the poems of *The Tower* and *The Winding Stair* Yeats applies all the force of his developed "metaphysical" style to summing up his past attitudes to life, to finding a formula which will indicate his present position while including all his past. The diversity and intensity of these poems, the recurring dominant images and themes and the constantly changing way in which they are treated, show us a great poet in the final period of his development gathering up his past into the present and attempting to find a comprehensive poetic attitude which will at once *include* all the past opposites and *free* him from them. That these volumes contain the fine flower of his poetry, few will deny. The poems are sometimes obscure, often difficult; they are poems to be read with concentrated attention if their full force and significance is to be appreciated, for though their most outstanding characteristic is power, it is not the power that hits the casual reader between the eyes so much as that which sings an ever fuller and richer note the more carefully the reader listens until it swells into a crashing harmony, complex yet unified, whose meaning seems to be now this, now that, never limited, always manifold, moving, suggestive, strangely ambiguous. When the strangeness and the ambiguity dominate, the poetry suffers; but when these qualities are allowed simply to play their part in filling out the overtones of the poem, in making the experience which the poem communicates as inclusive as possible, the result is wholly successful. To appreciate the best of these poems we do not need any detailed study of Yeats's prose works, though hints here and there are often very helpful; but we do need to know the dominant motives in Yeats's poetry, for the poems echo each other and often enrich each other in a very curious way. The two "Byzantium" poems, for example, should be read in sequence, "Sailing to Byzantium" first and then "Byzantium," for only thus can the full richness of the second poem be appreciated. But we need no knowledge from external sources to understand these two poems together; in fact the application of such knowledge will lessen the force of the poems by limiting their inclusiveness and leading us to interpret them too strictly in terms of what is after all a rather crazy esoteric system. That Yeats constructed his symbols on the basis of such a system is not relevant, for the full richness of a poem is rarely known to its creator, whose unconscious by-products are often as important as his conscious devices (Coleridge's poetry is a clear case in point). Further, there is a type of obscurity which enriches a poem rather than impoverishes it by giving suggestions of depth that cannot be produced in any other way. It is a very delicate balance to hold, and the unstable equilibrium between overprecision (which is limitation, exclusiveness, and thus impoverishment of the poem) and real obscurity (which is also impoverishment, through lack of any meaning) is extremely difficult to maintain. Yeats does not maintain it consistently, but he does play this difficult game with success surprisingly often. That it was a game which the eighteenth- and nineteenth-century poets rarely deigned to play at all suggests Yeats's importance in extending the scope of English poetry.

The Tower opens with "Sailing to Byzantium," where Yeats accepts his fate as an old man:

> That is no country for old men. The young
> In one another's arms, birds in the trees,
> —Those dying generations—at their song,
> The salmon-falls, the mackerel-crowded seas,
> Fish, flesh, or fowl, commend all summer long
> Whatever is begotten, born, and dies.
> Caught in that sensual music all neglect
> Monuments of unageing intellect.

There is a complex set of oppositions built up here—the old and the young, the physical and the mental, the changing and the permanent, the mortal and the immortal—in terms of which the thought of the poem is expressed. In the second stanza the contrast emerges as that between body and soul: an old man with a worn-out body "is but a paltry thing"

> . . . . unless
> Soul clap its hands and sing, and louder sing
> For every tatter in its mortal dress,

and so the poet has sailed to "the holy city of Byzantium," symbol of abstract intellect, of the "artifice of eternity" which is opposed to the changing natural world. Yet because the abstract intellect can construct the inclusive pattern which reconciles opposites it becomes something more than simply one side of the contrast—it is also the means of getting rid of the contrast.

The theme is developed again in "Byzantium," a poem in *The Winding Stair* volume. Here the oppositions are built into an even richer pattern; the images are more startling and more complex and the whole poem is more closely packed. Byzantium is now a state of mind, not a place, so the pairs of contrasting images are closer together than they were in "Sailing to Byzantium": in the midst of Ireland he is in Byzantium. The poet begins by dismissing the images of the natural life, of the life of change and violence whose symbol is the day (and the sun) as opposed to the night (and the moon):

> The unpurged images of day recede;
> The Emperor's drunken soldiery are abed.

The day is dismissed, and the silent night, symbol of abstract thought, of the changeless, the immortal, takes its place:

> A starlit or a moonlit dome disdains
> All that man is,
> All mere complexities,
> The fury and the mire of human veins.

In this mood the natural world—impure, violent, and changeable—becomes insignificant and the poet hails the superhuman, the abstract intellect that has no physical being:

> Before me floats an image, man or shade,
> Shade more than man, more image than a shade;
> For Hades bobbin bound in mummy-cloth
> May unwind the winding path.

The poem here is moving on toward the identification of the abstract intellect with death (a transition prepared for by the earlier identification of change and impurity with life). The undefinable being whom he hails is one who has already "climbed up the narrow winding stair to bed," one who has reached the top of the spiral and achieved unity and singleness through death. (We realize now that this top point of Yeats's spiral is death, not old age: the tower is crumbling at the top, for old age is fitly represented by a ruin, "half-dead at the top," but with death the symbol shifts from the ruined tower to the complete spiral.)

In the second stanza the poet achieves his identification with this symbol of abstract intellect (which is also death). This leads to the symbols of changelessness and abstraction in the following stanza's becoming at the same time symbols of artifice, which stands for permanence through death, as opposed to natural activity which represents life and change. The moon and the stars preside over these symbols of artifice and abstraction, for already in the first stanza they became symbols of the opposition to natural life. The "miracle, bird or golden handiwork" which can

> by the moon embittered, scorn aloud
> In glory of changeless metal
> Common bird or petal
> And all complexities of mire or blood

is a restatement in terms now developed by the movement of the poem of the earlier sentence,

> A starlit or a moonlit dome disdains
> All that man is.

In the second statement the poet is now identified with this attitude of scorn for the natural world of flesh and blood. He is now at the top point of the spiral, in the realm of changelessness, purity, and abstraction:

> At midnight on the Emperor's pavement flit
> Flames that no faggot feeds, nor steel has lit,
> Nor storm disturbs, flame begotten of flame.

Having thus identified himself with this midnight world of artifice, changelessness, and death, the poet can live out the remainder of his days untouched by the "complexities of mire or blood," the passions and changes of human life. He is in Ireland, yet he is of Byzantium; in the midst of life he is in death; he has become a spirit who sails over the flood of human life without even getting his feet wet by it:

> Astraddle on the dolphin's mire and blood,
> Spirit after spirit!

And the symbols of abstraction and artifice that he has created for himself preserve him from succumbing to the siren call of the human passions:

> Marbles of the dancing floor
> Break bitter furies of complexity,
> Those images that yet
> Fresh images beget,
> That dolphin-torn, that gong-tormented sea.

The "gong-tormented sea," human life torn by changing passions and emotions, seethes around his feet but can no longer reach him.

While in "Sailing to Byzantium" the contrasting images move farther and farther apart as the poem develops, the very reverse is true of "Byzantium," where the opposites, while remaining opposed, move ever closer together, until the poet is left an inhuman spirit in the very midst of human life. There is even a suggestion that the opposites are perhaps different aspects of the same thing. The last stanza can be interpreted in many different ways, and perhaps some readers will see a resolution of opposites there more definitely than others. For all through the poem Yeats uses ambiguity to provide depth and implication, and haunting phrases like "gong-tormented sea" and "miracle, bird or golden handiwork" can be interpreted indefinitely.

This account of the "Byzantium" poems is not meant as a statement of the whole truth about them, but simply as an indication of the possibilities of interpretation. One could interpret "Byzantium" very exactly and precisely in terms of Yeats's own esoteric system, quoting from his prose writings to show that the phases of the moon are referred to in this phrase and in that and indicating all kinds of parallels between the images of the poem and his theory of history, personality, and memory. But this kind of criticism by exclusion, by limitation, can never account for the impressiveness of the poem or explain its appeal. To explain a moving and impressive poem by a fantastic philosophy cannot be very satisfactory; that we have to do so with some of Yeats's poems, which admit of no more general interpretation, simply means that in those poems he is not successful.

It is Yeats's structural ability and his superb gift of phrase which enable him to transform private mutterings into great poetry. Many of his poems are so well designed and expressed with such a strange power that we are aware of a significant pattern before we know what the significance is. That is how we read "Byzantium" for the first time, and it is how we read some of his later plays whose significance often remains quite obscure.

The influence of Plotinus becomes increasingly noticeable in Yeats's later work. He seeks for a reality that lies outside time, and it is through this idea that he achieves the final resolution of his opposites. "Between extremities Man runs his course" and the problem is to destroy

> All those antinomies
> Of day and night.

If one could get outside time and outside memory, viewing all things simultaneously and at once, then one would have found the true pattern for reality—one could rest at the top of the spiral and see one's self on all parts of the winding stair at once. This search for an extra-temporal reality is reflected in numerous poems in *The Tower* and *The Winding Stair:*

> If I make the lashes dark
> And the eyes more bright
> And the lips more scarlet,
> Or ask if all be right
> From mirror after mirror,
> No vanity's displayed:
> I'm looking for the face I had
> Before the world was made.

and again,

> What can be shown?
> What true love be?
> All could be known or shown
> If Time were but gone.

"Time's filthy load" must be got rid of, and Yeats seems to have turned to the Plotinian "timeless individualities" for help in this problem.

> All lives that has lived;
> So much is certain;
> Old sages were not deceived:
> Somewhere beyond the curtain
> Of distorting days
> Lives that lonely thing
> That shone before these eyes
> Targeted, trod like Spring.

One important aspect of Byzantium is that it is a city without time.

Yeats wrote in 1931:

Plotinus . . . . was the first to establish as sole source the timeless individuality or daimon instead of the Platonic Idea, to prefer Socrates to his thought. This timeless individuality contains archetypes of all possible existences whether of man or brute, and as it traverses its circle of allotted lives, now one, now another, prevails. We may fail to express an archetype or alter it by reason, but all done from nature is its unfolding into time. Some other existence may take the place of Socrates, yet Socrates can never cease to exist. . . . . Plotinus said that we should not "baulk at the limitlessness of the intellectual; it is an infinitude having nothing to do with number or part" (*Ennead* V. 7. I.); yet it seems that it can at will re-enter number and part and thereby make itself apparent to our minds. If we accept this idea many strange or beautiful things become credible.[7]

This idea is to be found expressed in many different ways in Yeats's later poetry, and some of his groups of linked poems—"Words for Music Perhaps" and "A Woman Young and Old"—are essentially a series of myths exploring aspects of this Plotinian notion:

> That lover of a night
> Came when he would,
> Went into the dawning light
> Whether I would or no;
> Men come, men go;
> *All things remain in God.*

Crazy Jane and Tom the Lunatic are characters whose function is to show the inadequacy of orthodox philosophy; only the inspired or the mad can rend the veil of time and see all life as a unity. It is Crazy Jane who tells the moralizing bishop what he has been unable to find out for himself—

> 'Fair and foul are near of kin,
> And fair need foul,' I cried—

7 *Wheels and Butterflies* (New York, 1935), pp. 32–33.

and can explain the true relationship of the opposites by seeing them united outside time, while it is Tom the Lunatic who declares his faith in timeless individualities:

> Whatever stands in field or flood
> Bird, beast, fish or man,
> Mare or stallion, cock or hen,
> Stands in God's unchanging eye
> In all the vigour of its blood;
> In that faith I live or die.

Yeats's search for a complete and systematic symbolization of experience—originating in his desire to compensate for a no longer tenable religious tradition—finally led him to a highly abstract and artificial philosophy from which ordinary human values had almost completely disappeared. If he could not obtain adequate pattern from life, he would do so from death. The poetry of his last years becomes increasingly bloodless, though always skilful and often impressive, and sometimes we begin to wonder whether he is a man like ourselves or

> Shade more than man, more image than a shade.

Louis Macneice has charged him with "a constitutional inhumanity," and most readers of the very last poems of Yeats will understand why. There is a cold inhuman exultation in some of the *New Poems* (1938) and *Last Poems* (1939).

> The gyres! the gyres! Old Rocky Face look forth;
> Things thought too long can be no longer thought,
> For beauty dies of beauty, worth of worth,
> And ancient lineaments are blotted out.

We are a little scared of this rapt old man shouting strange cold words at us.

On September 4, 1938, he wrote a significant epitaph for himself:

> Under bare Ben Bulben's head
> In Drumcliffe churchyard Yeats is laid.
> An ancestor was rector there
> Long years ago, a church stands near,
> By the road an ancient cross.
> No marble, no conventional phrase;
> On limestone quarried near the spot
> By his command these words are cut:
> > *Cast a cold eye*
> > *On life, on death.*
> > *Horseman pass by.*

He was casting a very cold eye on life himself at this time. For over fifty years he sought for a philosophy to replace a lost tradition, that he might write better and with more confidence; and in the end his system conquered him. In his enthusiasm for the pattern that he was to impose upon experience he forgot about experience itself, so that while he retained his vigor he almost lost his humanity. In his last years his poetry was impressive but a little uncanny: he had cast too cold an eye on life.

CHAPTER IX

POETRY IN THE 1930'S. I: CECIL DAY LEWIS

WHILE Eliot was becoming more theological and more conservative with every new utterance and Yeats was patiently waiting for the phases of the moon to bring about the next phase in civilization, younger poets were emerging who were equally out of sympathy with both these attitudes. Eliot's didactic pessimism and Yeats's personal mythmaking were both rejected, for neither seemed to lead out of the Waste Land. Growing up in the aftermath of the first World War, these younger poets saw the Waste Land not only as a mental state but also as a physical condition which included industrial stagnation, unemployment, poverty—

> Smokeless chimneys, damaged bridges, rotting wharves and choked canals,
> Tramlines buckled, smashed trucks lying on their side across the rails;
> Power-stations locked, deserted, since they drew the boiler fires;
> Pylons falling or subsiding, trailing dead high-tension wires.[1]

The lack of a tradition, the disintegration of the old systems, that had worried Yeats and Eliot worried these poets, too; but, what the two older poets never did, they related this lack and this disintegration to the physical condition of their country. They therefore looked for a revolution both spiritual and physical,

[1] W. H. Auden.

190

which would at once revitalize tradition and cure the social and economic ills of their time.

It was no slick panacea that these poets offered, and indeed to conceive of them as writing propaganda poetry to advocate remedies is grossly to simplify and to misunderstand their whole position. They were faced with complex problems as poets as well as men. Having become conscious of something like a break in the English poetic tradition at the very outset of their careers, they were faced with problems of communication that threatened to inhibit their poetic progress completely. The problem of communication was closely bound up with the problem of attitude; if they could make up their minds how they ought to face the civilization of their day, they would know to whom they were speaking and through what symbols to express themselves. Aesthetic and political problems became very closely related, for before they could determine their own function as poets they had to come to some conclusion concerning their relation to the society of their time, and this conclusion was bound to have political implications. There was also the question of audience. The disintegration of the audience for poetry—one aspect of the breakdown of common value criteria and the dispersion of public belief that we have several times referred to—meant that the poet was now faced with the very difficult decision: *for whom* was he going to write. The problems of determining attitude and finding an audience are not really distinct; once you have decided on the former, you will find that the latter has been decided for you, and the section of the public to which you address yourself will have to be that which is either sympathetic to the attitude you have adopted or capable of being rendered sympathetic. A young left-wing poet using a combination of the techniques of Hopkins and Eliot in discussing the diseased condition of contemporary society would have no appeal to those who identified poetry with the Tennysonian tradition and would be read by few who did not accept the premise that radical change was desirable and inevitable.

What to say, how to say it, and to whom to say it were thus the three very closely interrelated problems that faced the young poet who began his career at the end of the 1920's. In the work of Cecil Day Lewis, W. H. Auden, and Stephen Spender we can see how these problems were tackled and what the results were for English poetry. Between 1929 and 1934 these poets had produced sufficient work from a more or less common standpoint to induce one of them—Cecil Day Lewis—to explain their work to the public in a short study with the significant title, *A Hope for Poetry*.

In his opening chapter Day Lewis states that "post-war poetry was born amongst the ruins," and he claims as its ancestors Hopkins, Owen, and Eliot, indicating that through Eliot the influence of the French Symbolists, of the Elizabethan dramatists, and of John Donne was also transmitted to the post-war poets. Hopkins was "discovered" by a small section of the English literary public during the years that followed the publication of his work by Bridges in 1918, and his influence on the younger poets soon became noticeable. That constant unstable equilibrium of Hopkins' verse, that violent attempt to wrest language to the expression of a complex yet fierce emotion that we find so often in his work, were qualities that made a natural appeal to young poets who had rejected altogether the Tennysonian method of handling language and who at the same time felt an urgent need to express an emotion that was driving in several directions at once. For the same reason they took over the "metaphysical" irony of Eliot and something of the technique of the seventeenth-century poets, a technique that enabled the poet to fuse several opposing attitudes into one, to remain constantly aware of alternative approaches to the situation—and thus a technique likely to be adopted by writers who were searching among many attitudes for a position and an audience.

If Eliot and Yeats were disturbed by the lack of a living tradition in their time, it is to be expected that these younger poets would be even more distressed. And indeed they were: "The Great War tore away our youth from its roots," Day Lewis tells us, and the problem of "re-establishing communication with the past" became urgent. Because the process had gone so much further than it had when Yeats and Eliot began writing, these poets could not be content with finding a personal compensation for the Waste Land (and in any case a personal compensation was less possible at this time). They sought first of all for a clear understanding of what had happened, for a history of the process which had brought about the present situation, and for a plan for the future which such an understanding could bring them. Neither Yeats nor Eliot had turned their eyes to the future. Eliot sought the ideal in an earlier age of belief, while Yeats sought it within his

own mind, content to wait until the inevitable movement of history brought about a new state of affairs.
But for Lewis, Auden, and Spender the situation was
more desperate. They saw their country as diseased
and demanding immediate cure. "What do you think
about England, this country of ours where nobody is
well?" asks the prize-day speaker in Auden's *Orators*,
and the question is fundamental in the poetry of all
three poets.

They were looking to the past for understanding and
to the future for remedy. What, after all, was the English tradition? Perhaps if they could understand it
properly and interpret it aright, they would find that
it had not really dried up but had gone underground
somewhere, ready to come to the surface again if only
they knew what the formula was whose pronounce-
ment would cause it to emerge. Perhaps those aspects
of tradition which had become a useless mockery did
not really represent the vital tradition of their civilization. Perhaps the pessimists misunderstood the past,
and so misinterpreted the present and had all the
wrong expectations about the future. For these poets
did not thrust the past behind them and turn with
utopian zeal to a vision of the future; they tried to find
a way of carrying the past into the future, of combining
tradition with revolution. Day Lewis, in *A Hope for Poetry*, quotes Spender's poem beginning

I think continually of those who were truly great

and comments: "I see in this poem a successful attempt to re-establish communication with the past, a
minor miracle of healing. And it takes the form of an-

cestor worship." And he cites in this connection Auden's search for his "real ancestors."

What does all this mean? It means that here we have a group of poets whose most immediate feeling is that of having been torn up by the roots. As poets they are uncertain about their audience, their function, their attitude, their means of expression. And as men they see themselves cut off from the past of their civilization in a world where the twin evils of social misery and spiritual barrenness are prevalent. Their aim is to understand the past, interpret the present, plan for the future. They must discover an attitude which reflects all three aspects of their aim, a language whose symbols can communicate on all three levels, an audience to whom they can make themselves understood. They search for roots, not in order to bury themselves in the earth but in order to be able to grow up into the sun. They desire to establish contact with the past so that they can go forward confidently into the future. Thus we shall find in their poetry a curious mixture of symbols of tradition and symbols of revolution. Hope is derived from the past and from the future; from the present are derived only symbols of disease, impetus to change—

> England our cow
> Once was a lady—is she now?[2]

Cecil Day Lewis, born in 1904, is the oldest of these three poets. His three groups of poems, *Transitional Poem* (1929), *From Feathers to Iron* (1931), and *The Magnetic Mountain* (1933)[3] show the development of an

[2] W. H. Auden.

[3] Published together as *Collected Poems, 1929–1933* by the Hogarth Press, London, 1935.

attitude, the progress from confusion to coherence, that is typical of all these writers. The theme of *Transitional Poem* he himself gives as "the single mind." "The poem is divided into four phases of personal experience in the pursuit of single-mindedness: it will be seen that a transition is intended from one part to the next such as implies a certain spiritual progress and a consequent shifting of aspect."[4] This "pursuit of single-mindedness" represents an attempt on the part of the poet to ascertain his own position; it is a preliminary feeling for an attitude. The commentary is to be found in *A Hope for Poetry*, where Day Lewis writes: "Standing at the end of an epoch, the poet's arms are stretched out to opposite poles, the old life and the new; that is his power and his crucifixion. . . . . Standing as a man between two worlds, he stands as a poet between two fires." There is a certain obscurity in *Transitional Poem* arising from this search for an attitude; the poet moves swiftly from point to point, from mood to mood, in a restless search for a landing-place. Like Yeats and Eliot he is searching for order—

> Now I have come to reason
> And cast my schoolboy clout,
> Disorder I see is without . . . .
> It is certain we shall attain
> No life till we stamp on all
> Life the tetragonal
> Pure symmetry of brain.

But unlike the earlier poets, he regards his search for mental order as preliminary to a plan of action.

The first part of *Transitional Poem* is a series of discussions of general philosophical problems conducted

[4] *Collected Poems*, p. 55.

from a constantly shifting point of view and through ever changing fables. There is no conclusion, no resolution of the separate statements. The second part is concerned with the problem of right action; the poet is seeking to find out where he ought to offer loyalty, what ethical system should command his allegiance:

> It is becoming now to declare my allegiance,
> To dig some reservoir for my springtime's pain,
> Bewilderment and pride, before their insurgence
> Is all sopped up in this dry regimen.

The preface to this section is a significant quotation from Whitman:

> Do I contradict myself?
> Very well then, I contradict myself;
> I am large, I contain multitudes.

The discussions in this second part are as unfocused as those in the first. The poet proceeds from speculation to speculation. The tentative quality of the thought is even more apparent here:

> In heaven, I suppose, lie down together
> Agonised Pilate and the boa-constrictor
> That swallows anything: but we must seize
> One horn or the other of our antitheses.
> When I consider each independent star
> Wearing its world of darkness like a fur
> And rubbing shoulders with infinity,
> I am content experience should be
> More discontinuous than the points pricked
> Out by the mazy course of a derelict,
> Iceberg, or Flying Dutchman, and the heart
> Stationary and passive as a chart. . . . . ,
>
> But an eccentric hour may come, when systems
> Not stars divide the dark; and then life's pistons
> Pounding into their secret cylinder
> Begin to tickle the most anchorite ear

With hints of mechanisms that include
The man. And once that rhythm arrests the blood,
Who would be satisfied his mind is no
Continent but an archipelago? . . . .

The questions are left unanswered, the moral problems suggested are not solved, but the section ends with an acceptance of experience, of life, as the best position to take up while deciding:

Charabancs shout along the lane
And summer gales bay in the wood
No less superbly because I can't explain
What I have understood.

Let logic analyse the hive,
Wisdom's content to have the honey:
So I'll bite the crust of things and thrive
While hedgerows still are sunny.

This confident acceptance of the natural world is something far removed from anything we find in Eliot and is an indication of the direction which the younger poets are to take. Their criticisms, at least in their early poetry, are based on an underlying optimism.

The third part of *Transitional Poem* is concerned with the more general psychological problem of keeping the personality integrated and unified during the process of search and opens with a quotation from Herman Melville: "But even so, amid the tornadoed Atlantic of my being, do I myself still centrally disport in mute calm." This is the ideal rather than the actual situation. Again there is the same rapid movement from point to point, only this time the search is for a common denominator, as it were. There is the rejection of all factors that represent only a part of the personality:

> Farewell again to this adolescent moon;
>   I say it is a bottle
> For papless poets to feed their fancy on.

And there is the search for the integrating unit:

> Where is the true, the central stone
> That clay and vapour zone,
> That earthquakes budge nor vinegar bites away,
> That rivets man against Doomsday?

The final section of the poem is, in the poet's own words, "an attempt to relate the poetic impulse with the experience as a whole." It is perhaps the most difficult section of the poem to see as a whole; the ambiguity of the symbols, the tentative nature of the fables, suggest more than they explain: it seems clear that the poet is not yet in a position to make any summing up. It is, in fact, a "transitional poem," in which all meaning is bound to be in some degree ambiguous and all symbols ambivalent. Throughout the whole poem the writing is somewhat loose, even at times sloppy. Day Lewis is too often content to surrender his language completely to the casual wanderings of his mind so that his poetry lacks the cogency that comes from discipline.

Day Lewis' next group of poems, *From Feathers to Iron*, which expresses the poet's thoughts and emotions during the nine months before the birth of his first child, has more organization than *Transitional Poem*, for there is a central theme running through the whole to which all the parts are clearly related. But its general nature is similar to that of the earlier group. A number of mental and emotional situations are expressed which indicate a feeling for an attitude, a gathering-up of experience preparatory to a declaration of faith. There is a greater confidence in *From Feathers to Iron*, less of that tentative quality we noted in *Transitional Poem*, but the basis of that confidence is not yet made clear. The constant reference to the approaching birth of his child gives the poem a center that pulls the speculations into some sort of pattern. The note of hope sounds louder:

> More than all else might you,
> My son, my daughter,
> Be metal to bore through
> The impermeable clay
> And rock that overlay
> The living water.
>
> This way the waste land turns
> To arable, and towns
> Are rid of drought.

In *Transitional Poem* the poet was mainly concerned with adjusting himself to the present, with integrating his own personality before announcing any purpose. But here, with the child as the symbol of the future, and of hope in the future, he is beginning to look forward, to wonder, and to plan:

> It is time to think of you,
> Shortly will have your freedom.
> As anemones that renew
> Earth's innocence, be welcome. . . . .
>
> Is it here we shall regain
> Companionship? Here awakes
> A white hope shall preserve
> From flatterers, pimps and fakes
> Integrity and nerve?

We begin to see that combination of interpretation of the past, diagnosis of the present, and plan for the future that is so common in the work of Auden:

> Draw up conditions—will the heir conform?
> Or thank us for the favour, who
> Inherits a bankrupt firm,
> Worn-out machinery, an exhausted farm?

(We may note incidentally that here are the half-rhymes of Wilfred Owen, which are to be found frequently in the poetry of the 1930's.)

The optimism and the confidence grows as the poem draws near its conclusion:

> Hére too fountains will soon be flowing,
> Empty the hills where love was lying late, was playing,
> Shall spring to life: we shall find there
> Milk and honey for love's heir,
> Shadow from sun also, deep ground for growing.

The sequence ends with a lyric celebrating the birth, symbol of hope in the future:

> Come out in the sun, for a man is born to-day!

In *The Magnetic Mountain* Day Lewis has finally defined his position; his interpretation of past and present has been achieved, his own psychological conflicts have been resolved, and he sets out in singleness of purpose to express his new faith and his new program. The revolutionary optimism that runs through the poem is indicated by the quotation from Rex Warner prefixed to the first part:

> Come, then, companions, this is the spring of blood,
> Heart's heyday, movement of masses, beginning of good.

There is a unity in the images that run through the poem that we do not find at all in *Transitional Poem* and find to a much less degree in *From Feathers to Iron*. The image of the kestrel, symbol of hope and enthusiasm, is found in the very first lines—

> Now to be with you, elate, unshared,
> My kestrel joy, O hoverer in wind—

and recurs continually. The lyrical quality is more certain than in the earlier poems, for the poet is now speaking from a unified personality and in expressing himself he is creating a pattern.

The magnetic mountain is the symbol of the new world that is to be created, a world that draws to itself the hopes of the present generation, though the road to it has never been charted:

> Somewhere beyond the railheads
> Of reason, south or north,
> Lies a magnetic mountain
> Riveting sky to earth.

This is to be the solution to the problem of contemporary chaos:

> Oh there's a mine of metal,
> Enough to make me rich
> And build right over chaos
> A cantilever bridge.

The confidence, the lyrical quality, the lack of obscurity of *The Magnetic Mountain* as compared to Day Lewis' earlier poetry do not arise solely from his having made up his mind, integrated his personality; he has also found his audience and knows to whom he is speaking. His audience consists of those younger writers who share his ideal:

> Wystan, Rex, all of you that have not fled,
> This is our world, this is where we have grown
> Together in flesh and live; though each alone
> Shall join the enclosed order of the dead,
> Enter the silent brotherhood of bone.

This appeal to Wystan Auden and Rex Warner, and the reference to the "silent brotherhood," indicates that the poet has found not only unity within himself but a sense of identity with a group outside of himself. Both are necessary before a poet can write with real confidence. The patterns of the individual lyrics now become more coherent, more self-explanatory; the form is at once more elaborate and more intelligible, for now that the frame of reference has been fixed a much more complicated poetic dialectic is possible without any danger of obscurity. The obscurity of parts of *Transitional Poem* arose from confusion, not from complexity.

The influence of Auden is very noticeable. The fourth lyric of the first part, with its breezy catalogue of symbolic contemporary figures, suggests Auden at once:

> Make no mistake, this is where you get off,
> Sue with her suckling, Cyril with his cough,
> Bert with a blazer and a safety-razor,
> Old John Braddleum and Terence the toff.
> And now, may I ask, have you made any plans?
> You can't go further along these lines.

And the conclusion of this lyric expresses his unity with his fellow-poets, who had already reached this point:

> Then I'll hit the trail for that promising land;
> May catch up with Wystan and Rex my friend,
> Go mad in good company, find a good country,
> Make a clean sweep or make a clean end.

Added vitality is given to the poem by the introduction of a dramatic element in the second part: the first and second defendants speak for the doomed world while the poet speaks for the future. This dramatic

element is another indication that the poet has found
his own position, for not until he knows where he
stands himself can he afford to introduce the voice of
the enemy. In Part III the speeches of the four
enemies keep the drama alive, while the poet's own
position is defined more clearly. Gradually the revolutionary implications of the poem fill out, and it becomes clear that the poet is demanding a clean sweep
of the corrupt old order and the building of a socialist
world:

> It is now or never, the hour of the knife,
> The break with the past, the major operation.

The tone of the poem is by no means one of exultant
optimism throughout. The poet is sizing up the
chances of cure, glancing from the present to the future
and back again to the present. Sometimes the present
only depresses:

> Comrades, my tongue can speak
> No comfortable words,
> Calls to a forlorn hope,
> Gives work and not rewards. . . . .

> Father, who endest all,
> Pity our broken sleep;
> For we lie down with tears
> And waken but to weep.

> And if our blood alone
> Will melt this iron earth,
> Take it. It is well spent
> Easing a saviour's birth.

Sometimes the mood is one of doubt and hesitation:

> Junction or terminus—here we alight.
> A myriad tracks converge on this moment,
> This man where all ages and men are married,
> Who shall right him? Who shall determine?

But all the variations of mood and tone are at bottom aspects of a single attitude, not gropings toward an attitude as they were in *Transitional Poem*. The structure is complicated and well knit, and as the poem progresses to its conclusion the resolution draws in sight:

> You that love England, who have an ear for her music,
> The slow movement of clouds in benediction,
> Clear arias of light thrilling over her uplands,
> Over the chords of summer sustained peacefully;
> Ceaseless the leaves' counterpoint in a west wind lively,
> Blossom and river rippling loveliest allegro,
> And the storms of wood strings brass at year's finale:
> Listen. Can you not hear the entrance of a new theme?

This is that reconciliation of traditional with revolutionary themes which Day Lewis, Spender, and Auden all strive after. It prepares for the triumphant conclusion:

> Beckon O beacon, and O sun be soon!
> Hollo, bells, over a melting earth!
> Let man be many and his sons all sane,
> Fearless with fellows, handsome by the hearth.
> Break from your trance: start dancing now in town,
> And, fences down, the ploughing match with mate.
> This is your day: so turn, my comrades, turn
> Like infants' eyes like sunflowers to the light.

In *A Time To Dance and Other Poems* (1935) we find Day Lewis expressing variations of the same attitude that we find in *The Magnetic Mountain*. The issue is seen as somewhat more specific, but it is the same issue, expressed with forceful clarity. The revolution is imminent:

> Who between town and country dreams of contact
>   with the two worlds
> Earthquake will wake, a chasm at his feet, crack of
>   doom overhead.

The first part of the volume consists of a number of individual lyrics expressing aspects of the situation as they affect either the author or the country in general. In "The Conflict" he describes his own emotion in the face of the future:

> I sang as one
> Who on a tilting deck sings
> To keep their courage up, though the wave hangs
> That shall cut off their sun. . . . .
>
> Singing I was at peace. . . . .
>
> Yet living here,
> As one between two massing powers I live
> Whom neutrality cannot save
> Nor occupation cheer.

And again we have the attempt to reconcile the past and the future, the English tradition and the English future:

> In me two worlds at war
> Trample the patient flesh,
> This lighted ring of sense where clinch
> Heir and ancestor.

The reconciliation of these two symbols—heir and ancestor—is an even more dominant theme in the poetry of W. H. Auden.

After these ten poems, which constitute the first part of the book, comes the title-poem, "A Time To Dance," entitled by Day Lewis "a symphonic poem" and inscribed to the memory of L. P. Hedges. The opening expresses confidence, celebration—

> My friend who within me laughs
> bids you dance and sing.

He bears a message of triumph from his dead friend:

> Let us sing then for my friend not a dirge, not a funeral
> anthem,
> But words to match his mirth, a theme with a happy end.

And he proceeds to sing in vigorous and triumphant language of the epic flight from England to Australia of Parer and M'Intosh, who flew the whole distance in January, 1920, in a tiny, obsolete machine. This little epic is perhaps the finest verse Day Lewis has written: rapid, lively, exciting, it carries forward the story in such a way as to keep the reader's interest at a high pitch throughout. But when the story has been told, the mood of triumph begins to ebb. The tempo of the verse changes and takes on an elegiac movement, concerned at first with sad reminiscence of his dead friend and gradually being extended to include a lament for the present state of civilization:

> So I returned. Perhaps he was nearer home
> And I had missed him. Here he was last seen
> Walking familiar as sunlight a solid road;
> Round the next turn, his door. But look, there has been
> Landslide: those streets end abruptly, they lead
> The eye into a tomb.

The elegy continues, moving again toward cheerfulness—

> Sirs, be merry: these are his funeral games—

until the other note emerges once again in the reply of those who have been asked to dance:

> Then a voice arose in the land, and an indignation
> from among the people,
> Saying, "Who is he that calls us to dance whose
> dancing days are over:

That bids us follow the free passage of ocean flyers
   when the slag-tip is our dead horizon and our
   days recur like a conveyor-belt bringing nothing
   new:
That mocks, with flash talk of the spirit outshining
   death, us who never received a permit to live?"
And I looked, and it was so.

There follows a series of pictures of the contemporary scene, showing industrial stagnation, unemployment, poverty, misery, hopelessness. These are made more poignant by being cast into the form of parodies of well-known lyrics or nursery rhymes:

Come live with me and be my love
And we will all the pleasures prove
Of peace and plenty, bed and board,
That chance employment may afford.

I'll handle dainties on the docks
And thou shalt read of summer frocks:
At evening by the sour canals
We'll hope to hear some madrigals.

They possess a grim effectiveness:

Oh hush thee, my baby,
Thy cradle's in pawn:
No blankets to cover thee
Cold and forlorn.
The stars in the bright sky
Look down and are dumb
At the heir of the ages
Asleep in a slum.

The poem then proceeds to a statement, in several different ways, of the revolutionary position, but expressed always as love, not as hate. It is his love for mankind, not his hatred of the oppressor, that provides his prime motive:

Love, love in action
Is best for me.

"Love in action" is the revolution. From music-hall doggerel to serious speculation and prophecy the poem works to its final conclusion, a union of pessimism and optimism, counting the cost yet with the certainty of ultimate victory. *A Time To Dance* is the most mature statement of Day Lewis' revolutionary position. At the time when it was written (1934) it represented the view of a large number of British intellectuals, particularly of those who had grown up after 1918.

Day Lewis next expressed his position in a prose pamphlet, *Revolution in Writing*, where he explained his view of the function of the artist in the contemporary situation. Then, in *Noah and the Waters*, a verse play written in 1936 something in the manner of the medieval moralities, he expressed in an allegorical manner the doom of the reactionaries and the necessary triumph of the socialist revolution. As the author put it, "The issue is the choice that must be made by Noah between clinging to his old life and trusting himself to the Flood." The play is developed "in a mixture of poetry, doggerel and rhetoric" and the allegory is of the simplest kind. It is significant as showing Day Lewis no longer addressing himself only to his fellow-intellectuals, his friends Auden and Rex Warner, but seeking for the wider audience provided by the stage. There were many poets at this time—Eliot and Auden among them—who were turning to popular verse drama as a means of regaining an audience for poetry.

In 1938 Day Lewis published *Overtures to Death and Other Poems*, and by this time a lot of water had flowed under the bridge since the appearance of his last collection. Fascism had made great strides in Europe. The

Franco rebellion in Spain was drawing to its ill-omened victory, helped by "nonintervention." A European war seemed certain, sooner or later. The revolutionary confidence and hope have disappeared from Day Lewis' poetry, and though the note of encouragement is occasionally struck, as in the poem "In the Heart of Contemplation," it is not the dominant one. "February 1936" is full of a bitter foreboding:

> We cannot meet
> Our children's mirth, at night
> Who dream their blood upon a darkening street.
>
> Stay away, Spring!
> Since death is on the wing
> To blast our seed and poison everything.

The note of warning replaces the note of optimism:

> See the big guns, rising, groping, erected
> To plant death in your world's soft womb.
> Fire-bud, smoke-blossom, iron seed projected—
> Are these exotics? They will grow nearer home:
>
> Grow nearer home—and out of the dream-house
>   stumbling
> One night into a strangling air and the flung
> Rags of children and thunder of stone niagaras
>   tumbling,
> You'll know you slept too long.

The sequence of poems that gives the volume its title, "Overtures to Death," is a group of seven poems in which the poet addresses Death in a variety of moods. They are strange and disturbing poems, and the outcome of them all is that Death is now a permanent guest in the modern world:

> For us, born into a still
> Unsweetened world, of sparse

Breathing-room, alleys brackish as hell's pit
And heaven-accusing spires,

You were never far nor fable,
Judgement nor happy end:
We have come to think of you, mister, as
Almost the family friend.

It is strange and disturbing to see the former prophet of
a new life turning to hobnob with Death, and it is
symptomatic of a change that was coming over British
consciousness in the last years of the 1930's. The delay
in getting things done, the acquiescence in evil, the
placid waiting for the coming terror, move the poet
sometimes to despair, sometimes to anger, sometimes
to desperate exhoration:

Do you need the horn in your ear, the hounds at your heel,
Gadflies to sting you sore,
The lightning's angry feint, and all
The horizon clouds boiling like lead, before
You'll risk your javelin dive
And pierce reflection's heart, and come alive?

And, as though by way of heroic example, he includes
a long narrative poem, "The Nabara," which gives a
stirring account of the sea fight between three Basque
government trawlers and the rebel cruiser "Canarias."
It is well told—Day Lewis can do this sort of thing
excellently—and the moral emerges clear and passionate. The little Basque trawlers were smashed to bits,
their crews slaughtered almost to a man (the "Nabara," which fought to the end, went down fighting,
and no member of the crew survived) in this fight
against overwhelming odds. The conclusion is tragic,

yet comforting, and the faith of these Basque sailors is contrasted with that of the politicians:

Freedom was more than a word, more than the base coinage
Of politicians who hiding behind the skirts of peace
They had defiled, gave up that country to rack and carnage . . . .
For these I have told of, freedom was flesh and blood—a mortal
Body, the gun-breech hot to its touch: yet the battle's height
Raised it to love's meridian and held it awhile immortal . . . .

The volume concludes with "Self-criticism and Answer," where he at first doubts the efficacy of his "too meticulous words"; but he answers himself in the last verse, which is his last word in the book:

When madmen play the piper
And knaves call the tune,
Honesty's a right passion—
She must call to her own.
Let yours be the start and stir
Of a flooding indignation
That channels the dry heart deeper
And sings through the dry bone.

Overtures to Death is an angry and sometimes bitter volume, more various in its themes than any since *Transitional Poem*. The single-minded confidence that we see in *The Magnetic Mountain* and *Noah and the Waters* is now much less in evidence, and the unified personality that the poet had sought and found in his earlier work is threatening to disintegrate again. But this collection contains his best poetry. The mixture of bitterness and hope, of blame and encouragement, of futility and determination, makes for richer moods and more complex poems than the earlier single strain. The too easy style of his earlier poetry, which seemed to flow with excessive smoothness, has given way to a more subtly cadenced and carefully balanced verse. In his very earliest period Day Lewis was content to slap down his diverse and contradictory thoughts as they came, and the poetry thus lacked depth and unity. In his next period, though unity is there and the poet's new-found attitude helps him to shape his verse with more confidence, there is a certain narrowness, a certain oversimplicity in the poetical argument, resulting from the naïveté of the convert, though it is true that he does develop certain types of dramatic complexity at this time. But in the third period the drama is within himself, not between himself and symbolic enemies set up to be knocked down. "Out of our quarrel with others we make rhetoric," Yeats once said, "but out of our quarrel with ourselves, poetry." Day Lewis has to adjust his revolutionary attitude to the contradictions and the tragedies of a world being slowly strangled by fascism, and the result is a less facile poetry. For facility had been the greatest fault of his earlier work. But with *Overtures to Death* we find a new discipline and richness of phrase that comes from a complex yet unified emotion:

> You leaves drenched with the lifeblood of the year—
> What flamingo dawns have wavered from the east,
> What eves have crimsoned to their toppling crest
> To give the fame and transience that you wear!
> Leaf-low he shall lie soon: but no such blaze
> Briefly can cheer man's ashen, harsh decline;
> His fall is short of pride, he bleeds within
> And paler creeps to the dead end of his days.
> O light's abandon and the fire-crest sky
> Speak in me now for all who are to die!

CHAPTER X

POETRY IN THE 1930'S. II: W. H. AUDEN AND STEPHEN SPENDER

THE poetic development of W. H. Auden (born in 1907) parallels in many ways that of Day Lewis. Both poets begin by feeling for an attitude and for an audience and acquiring confidence and clarity as they find them. In some respects the dilemma of the English poet in the 1930's is more clearly indicated in Auden's work than in that of any of his contemporaries. We can see there particularly clearly the relation between the question of what symbols to employ and that of what public to address.

Auden's first volume, *Poems* (1930), shows a great number of contemporary influences conflicting with each other. On his actual technique, the principal influences are Hopkins, Eliot, Anglo-Saxon poetry, Skelton, and Wilfred Owen. His point of view hovers between Marx and Freud, discussing the contemporary situation at one time as a Marxist observer, at another time as a clinical psychologist. The illness of the modern world is to be interpreted sometimes as an economic disease and sometimes as the symptom of a diseased state of mind. And in addition to this confusion between two diagnoses we find a confusion concerning the section of the public to whom the appeal is to be made. Whom should he take into his confidence, who shall determine his choice of symbols? "Comrade"

has a cheering sound to those who agree that we ought
to get together and do something to improve social
conditions, but to those who do not share this view it
is a distasteful word, suggesting Marxist dogma at its
most violent. When Auden says

> Make me some fresh tea, fetch me some rugs,

we understand this as a symbol of social futility only if
we share his assumptions about the nature of contemporary society.

Auden himself seems to be conscious of this difficulty
(he is perhaps the most self-conscious of all the contemporary poets). As a result, his symbolism wavers:
sometimes he is addressing a group of his personal
friends and using symbols intelligible to them alone,
and at other times he is addressing an indeterminate
audience, using symbols some of which are broadly
enough based to have a fairly wide appeal but others
of which are carried over from the first group and are
therefore only confusing. The attitude expressed in the
poems wavers similarly. The comparative obscurity of
the charade *Paid on Both Sides* arises from the fact that
Auden himself had not thought through the ideas he
intended it to express. Poem after poem indicates that
the author is searching for his own standpoint:

> Here am I, here are you:
> But what does it mean? What are we going to do?

The dissatisfaction with the present state of society is
indicated clearly and consistently, but there are only
vague and conflicting hints as to what is to be done
about it. And whom is he addressing? Who is it that
has to take this action? It is "we" and not "they,"

"they" being modern decadents and hypochondriacs, and "we" being—who? The very structure of the poems, such as the one beginning "Since you are going to begin to-day" with the swift transition from point to point of one who is searching for his own standpoint, indicates this uncertainty. As we read through a volume a few prevailing ideas emerge. "Death of the old gang" is a necessity (but the "old gang" is a highly ambiguous symbol), invalids and decadents, who are all regarded as shamming (which conflicts with his view that society is really diseased), must be pulled out of their Bath chairs, and all kinds of psychological maladjustment must be rectified. On the whole, these poems give the impression of a man of genuine poetic gifts possessing in a high degree the power to do new things with words who is not quite sure what he wants to say, and who is even less decided about whom he wants to address. The latter problem, we feel, is the more urgent: once he finds his audience—either a real or an ideal audience; it does not matter which, for the problem is simply to give consistency to his symbolisim and coherence to his attitude—he will be able to speak more clearly.

The prevailing theme in the 1930 volume is the futility of English upper-middle-class existence, expressed sometimes through direct description, sometimes through illustrative myth or fable created for the purpose and not always clear because of an ambiguous frame of reference. He is at his best in a diction which combines an easy colloquialism with a certain quiet formality:

Since you are going to begin to-day
Let us consider what it is you do.
You are the one whose part it is to lean,
For whom it is not good to be alone.
Laugh warmly turning shyly in the hall
Or climb with bare knees the volcanic hill,
Acquire that flick of wrist and after strain
Relax in your darling's arms like a stone
Remembering everything you can confess,
Making the most of firelight, of hours of fuss.

The conclusion of this poem has an effective simplicity:

Others have tried it and will try again
To finish that which they did not begin:
Their fate must always be the same as yours,
To suffer the loss they were afraid of, yes,
Holders of one position, wrong for years.

Here he is talking in the language of the class he is denouncing; but he cannot always do this, for really he belongs to the "other side." Sometimes he indicates his opposition by employing a sneering familiar note:

Its no use raising a shout.
No, Honey, you can cut that right out.
I don't want any more hugs;
Make me some fresh tea, fetch me some rugs . . . .

At other times he attempts an impersonal dignity, which is not always successful—it is not easy to be dignified when balanced on a razor edge—but which on occasions achieves memorable verse:

Beams from a car may cross a bedroom wall,
They wake no sleeper; you may hear the wind
Arriving driven from the ignorant sea
To hurt itself on pane, on bark of elm
Where sap unbaffled rises, being spring;
But seldom this.

POETRY AND THE MODERN WORLD

We see this same quality in the strange and effective ending of poem No. XVI:

> We know it, we know that love
> Needs more than the admiring excitement of union,
> More than the abrupt self-confident farewell,
> The heel on the finishing blade of grass,
> The self-confidence of the falling root,
> Needs death, death of the grain, our death,
> Death of the old gang; would leave them
> In sullen valley where is made no friend,
> The old gang to be forgotten in the spring,
> The hard bitch and the riding-master,
> Stiff underground; deep in clear lake
> The lolling bridegroom, beautiful, there.

But more often the poet hesitates between dignity and familiarity, and the result is a scattering of energy that pulls the poem to pieces as the reader reads.

Though in trying to find symbols and fables to express the situation as a whole Auden is not often successful in his early poems, he does often achieve success in illuminating the individual impulse, the isolated emotion, whose function in the complete pattern is never very clear yet which has a separate effectiveness of its own. The impulse for sudden and adventurous action—favorite with Auden—flashes out every now and again:

> Where lights and wine are set
> For supper by the lake,
> But leaders must migrate:
> 'Leave for Cape Wrath to-night,'
> And the host after waiting
> Must quench the lamps and pass
> Alive into the house.

Or the sudden sense of futility and doom:

> For no one goes
> Further than railhead or the ends of piers,
> Will neither go nor send his son
> Further through foothills than the rotting stack
> Where gaitered gamekeeper with dog and gun
> Will shout 'Turn back.'

The attempt to sum up the modern situation in fables or through the arrangement of the proper symbols—an attempt resulting so often in obscurity, for the reasons we have discussed—is sometimes abandoned completely in favor of simple direct abuse or warning:

> Financier, leaving your little room
> Where the money is made but not spent,
> You'll need your typist and your boy no more;
> The game is up for you and for the others.

In the concluding poem he lists the contemporary evils in psychological not economic terms, asking God (whom he addresses as "Sir" in the manner of Hopkins) to send

> . . . . a sovereign touch
> Curing the intolerable neural itch,
> The exhaustion of weaning, the liar's quinsy,
> And the distortions of ingrown virginity.

The poem—in sonnet form—concludes with an appeal that God

> look shining at
> New styles of architecture, a change of heart,

in which the clash of symbols is deliberate and effective.

In the 1930 volume we see the poet as critic of his generation, expressing his criticism to a shifting audience and in shifting terms. With *The Orators* (1932) we have the next stage. Here we see Auden's dilemma more clearly still. The obscurity in this book—a collection of faintly related fables, some expressed dramatically, some lyrically, some rhetorically—is the obscurity of a poet who does not want to be obscure but cannot help himself: he is halfway between the private coterie and the public group in his search for an audience, and thus both his attitudes and his symbols will be Janus-faced, looking two ways. The three-line dedication to Stephen Spender is illuminating:

> Private faces in public places
> Are wiser and nicer
> Than public faces in private places.

He would rather write for a larger group in terms intelligible only to a smaller group, so that members of the smaller group will have the pleasant surprise of recognizing "private faces in public places," than employ the reverse method and run the risk of leveling his friends to the common state of apprehension of ordinary folk. That he should formulate his problem in terms of this alternative is significant.

In *The Orators* we see a destructive and a constructive purpose wrestling for supremacy. Sometimes Auden takes the line of least resistance and states the situation as a simple conflict between schoolboys and their teachers, or as a vague struggle between disease and health, the latter never being clearly defined. At other times he seeks to seize on more concrete aspects of the conflict. But always his mythmaking—and Auden's mythopoeic faculty is as strong in its way as that of Yeats, though quite different in character and employed for a wholly different purpose—is obscured by his doubts concerning the public for whom he is constructing his myths. (Yeats never doubted, for he was constructing his myths for himself only.) We can see some progress, however, toward the crystallization of attitude and audience. In the English public-school imagery of the "Address for a Prize-Day," with which *The Orators* opens, we see the first step forward in his decision to fight the public-school spirit with its own weapons. It is in the "Address," too, that we find the formulation of the theme of the whole book: "What do you think about England, this country of ours where nobody is well?" The "you" here are schoolboys: Auden is addressing the educated youth of his country. But the identity of the speaker is not yet fixed. The movement toward identifying his public with some kind of idealized conception of the schoolboy is illustrated not only by the predominant imagery of *The Orators* (imagery from school life, school sports, and O.T.C. activities) but also by the dedication of the second of the "Six Odes" (which constitute Book III of *The Orators*) to "Gabriel Carritt, Captain of Sedbergh School XV," of the fifth of the odes to his pupils, of the fourth to the young son of Rex Warner, and by the suggestion that salvation is to come from the young:

John, son of Warner, shall rescue you.

The Orators is probably, for the ordinary reader, the most obscure work that Auden has produced. The shifting point of view, the ambiguous symbols, the hero fading into villain and back again to hero (as in the "Journal of an Airman," the second book of *The Orators*), the abrupt transitions from one sort of fable to a totally different kind, all contribute to the reader's confusion. The subtitle, "An English Study," gives us some help, and the prologue epitomizes an underlying theme:

> Under the trees the summer bands were playing;
> 'Dear boy, be brave as these roots,' he heard them saying:
> Carries the good news gladly to a world in danger,
> Is ready to argue, he smiles, with any stranger.

> And yet this prophet, homing the day is ended,
> Receives odd welcome from the country he so defended:
> The band roars 'Coward, Coward,' in his human fever,
> The giantess shuffles nearer, cries 'Deceiver.'

But even this is to a certain extent ambiguous; we are unable to distinguish the straightforward from the ironical. "Dear boy" is the language of the upper-middle-class decadents against whom the poet is fighting: is the "dear boy" then the enemy, or is he the hero? The four verses of the prologue are open to two equal and opposite interpretations.

Book I opens in a straightforward manner: it is an attack on "the haters of life" conducted in public-school symbols:

> Now, boys, I want you all to promise me that you'll never be like that. Are you just drifting or thinking of flight? You'd better not. No use saying 'The mater wouldn't like it' or 'for my part I prefer to read Charles Lamb.' Need I remind you that you are no longer living in Ancient Egypt? Time's getting on and I must hurry or I shall miss my train. You've got some pretty stiff changes to make. . . . . I should like to see you make a beginning before I go, now, here. Draw up a list of rotters and slackers, of proscribed persons under headings like this. Committees for municipal or racial improvement—the headmaster. Disbelievers in the occult—the school chaplain. The bogusly cheerful—the games master—the really disgusted—the teacher of modern languages. All these have got to die without issue. Unless my memory

fails me there's a stoke hole under the floor of this hall, the Black Hole we called it in my day. New boys were always put in it. Ah, I see I am right. Well look to it. Quick, guard that door. Stop that man. Good. Now boys hustle them, ready, steady—go.

Though the general meaning of the address is plain, the reason for this particular selection of enemy qualities is never clear to the reader. There seems to be confusion emerging every now and again between personal grudges and the objective indictment of a way of life. Sometimes sheer horseplay is introduced as a sort of solvent of contradictory elements, but the result is rarely happy.

After the address follows another prose section entitled "Argument," where the images and symbols keep shifting with kaleidoscopic rapidity. The general theme seems to be (each reader must speak for himself here) purposive action emerging out of the Waste Land:

Lo, I a skull show you, exuded from dyke when no pick was by pressure of bulbs: at Dalehead a light moving, lanterns for lambing. Before the forenoon of discussion, as the dawn-guest wrinkles the pools, I waken with the idea of building.

A great number of symbols of the modern disease are introduced into this section, but they are not always distinguishable from symbols of cure. There follows an ironic appeal to the opiates of modern civilization— detective stories and pubs—made on behalf of those who show the symptoms of the contemporary malady. But here again we have the disturbing feeling that irony is developing into mere fun: the symbols won't stand still. And this section of Book I of *The Orators* concludes with another series of pictures representing aspects of the modern situation:

> Came one after a ruined harvest, with a school-room globe, a wizard, sorry. [This is Auden himself?] From the nipping North Righteousness running. But where that warm boy of the summer château? Found on wet roads early this morning, patches of oil, the face of an avenger, downwards. Speech of worn tools in a box, thoughts from the trap.
>
> Sound of guns in the city, the voice of the demonstrator, 'Gentlemen, tomorrow we shall tie the carotid.' What memory of self-regard from the locked room, shaken by lorries, from the depressed areas?

There follows another prose section, entitled simply "Statement," where Auden lists typical symptoms of the psychological disease of modern civilization. The fourth and final section of Book I is the extraordinary "Letter to a Wound," while Book II consists entirely of the bewildering "Journal of an Airman." Stephen Spender, who as a friend of Auden was presumably aware of Auden's intentions, has given some explanation of both of these:

> Those sections of *The Orators* called *Letters to a Wound* and *The Airman's Journal* are in some ways comparable to Rilke's *Notebook of Malte Laurids Brigge*. . . . . Rilke shared Auden's view of the psychological nature of illness. The view of both writers is, to summarize it crudely, that illness of the body is the physical expression of a defect of the mind: thus it is to be regarded with relief as a recognizable symptom, or even in some cases with gratitude as an effective cure, or as a means by which, through treatment of the body, a complicated illness of the mind may be relieved.[1]

Thus presumably the morbid cosy chat in which the writer of the "Letter to a Wound" indulges in address-

[1] Stephen Spender, *The Destructive Element* (London, 1938; 1st ed., 1935), pp. 264–65.

ing that wound which he hugs secretly to himself is a "recognizable symptom" of another aspect of the modern disease. Its precise function in *The Orators*, however, remains obscure. Of the "Journal" Spender has this to say:

. . . . The main interest of *The Airman's Journal* is how the airman is able to relate himself to society, and how far he is himself simply a product of the social life which has produced him.

The symbolic position of the airman is, as it were, to be on the margin of civilization. Being an airman, it is obvious that he is not tied down in any way; he is up in the air, and in the position of artists like Rilke or Lawrence who travel; and yet he is the man of action, flying, planning Fascist(?) coups, circulating leaflets. . . . . His chief danger is his remarkable irresponsibility which leads him to indulge in Fascist day-dreams of fantastic and murderous practical jokes. The airman, therefore, with his bird's eye view of society, sees everywhere the enemy. The most brilliant passages in the book are those in which he classifies the enemy.

We are never, of course, told directly who the enemy is, but only (i) how he behaves; (ii) symptoms by which we may recognize his influence on individuals; (iii) how, regarding him as a disease, we may recognize his symptoms in ourselves.[2]

Spender sums up his discussion of this section of *The Orators* with these observations:

The airman is particularly interesting because he is, in fact, in much the same position as the contemporary writer who hates the social system under which he exists, and lives, and writes in a dream of violence on behalf of himself and his friends. He is ignored by the greatest part of society, and neither directly nor indirectly does his work penetrate to it. Yet he may represent the most intelligent and critical forces in society. Supposing that he is living in a society that is self-destructive and actively preparing for war, he seems to be completely powerless. His elimination is *no loss* to society, as Fascist governments have discovered who have

[2] *Ibid.*, p. 268.

been able to dispose of all the groups representing culture in their countries, because this culture had no deep roots in the life of the people. The airman and the artist is, like Roderick Hudson, just dangerously and acutely himself, apart from the rest of the world, isolated in his sensibility. Yet without him civilization is only a name.

He has, therefore, like the airman, got to defeat the enemy. There are two methods of attack. The first is to become an active political agent, to take part in the immense practical joke of destruction. . . . . The second is to learn how he may escape from his own isolation; not to resist the enemy but to absorb him. To make an art that is infected by—that is about—society, and which it is impossible for society to discard, because it is essentially a part of it; and to make it a part which will transform the whole.[3]

There seems to be some confusion in Spender's thought here, and when we get similar ideas expressed through a constantly shifting fable in ambivalent symbols the confusion is extreme. There is some brilliant wit and observation in the "Journal of an Airman," but the pattern fails to shape itself into any real significance for the reader because of the poet's own doubts concerning his audience and (consequently) his symbols.

The "Six Odes," which represent the third and concluding book of *The Orators*, restate the general theme in a more personal manner, through discussion rather than through fable. In the fourth of these we get Auden's clearest expression of the psychological malady of his time and the kind of action that will cure it:

> See him take off his coat and get down with a spanner
> To each unhappy Joseph and repressed Diana,
> Say Bo to the invalids and take away their rugs,
> The war-memorials decorate with member-mugs,
> The gauche and the lonely he will introduce of course
> To the smaller group, the right field of force;

[3] *Ibid.*, pp. 273–74.

The few shall be taught who want to understand,
Most of the rest shall love upon the land;
Living in one place with a satisfied face
All of the women and most of the men
Shall work with their hands and not think again.

Just as Day Lewis gained hope and confidence for the future in celebrating the birth of his son, so Auden celebrates with optimism the birth of John Warner:

A birthday, a birth
On English earth
Restores, restore will, has restored
To England's story
The directed calm, the actual glory.

The Orators ends with an epilogue in which the timid and the apprehensive are dismissed from the group of those who look to the future.

A strange and in many ways an obscure work, *The Orators* is an interesting comment on the poet-public relation in the 1930's. With a combination of Freudian and Marxist ideas, Auden tries to construct a series of linked fables and discussions which will provide an interpretation of the modern world. His comparative failure results partly from the fact that he had not himself properly integrated these two sets of ideas and partly from his ambiguous position in regard to his readers.

There is a new simplicity of diction and symbolism in *The Dance of Death* (1933), a verse play in which the psychological diagnosis is for the time being dropped and the Marxist one alone applied. This in part explains the new simplicity, but there is another explanation too. In his journey from the coterie to a larger public Auden has now gone far enough to be less disturbed by the risk of "public faces in private places." Yet there is still uncertainty about the audience addressed. The allegory, a straightforward and obvious one in itself, is complicated in parts by a use of the old ambivalent imagery, which is the last thing one wants in a simple dramatic allegory. Auden may try to disguise this hesitancy as irony, but irony has no place in a direct sociopolitical parable, and its employment here is suspicious. It is all very well for Karl Marx to be deflated into a joke at the conclusion of the play, but for a poet who is about to deliver a message suddenly to lose confidence and indulge in horseplay instead indicates a confusion that does not conduce to poetic effectiveness. We so often see in the early Auden this combination of prophet and clown which is, perhaps, a natural refuge for a man in doubt about his audience.

In 1936 Auden published a collection of poems entitled *Look, Stranger* (in America, *On This Island*), and here we find the conflict to a large degree solved, at least temporarily. The simple and highly effective strain of description and meditation which runs through these poems, the subtle clarity and plastic handling of language which he displays, seem to indicate that at last he has found a public, that he knows to whom he is speaking. As a result both his attitude and his expression of attitude are clarified. His public, like the public envisaged by most poets, is in a sense an ideal one, yet sufficiently grounded in reality to provide him with a constant and impressive symbolism and a new strength of purpose. It might be called simply the ideal schoolboy. He is addressing those who will make the future, the alert youngster who observes his environment and is dissatisfied, and who requires more information about the present and direction for the future if he is to be able to do anything effective about it. Auden is demonstrating and illustrating and warning. There is the past, history and tradition, "our fathers"; there is the present, to be diagnosed; there is the future, to be built. All three are discussed as though in the presence of one who will have to do the rebuilding. This does not mean that all the poems are actually addressed to schoolboys, or even worded for that kind of an audience; it means simply that by envisaging that kind of audience he has been able to clarify both his own attitude and his use of symbols, and having attained that new clarification he can write to whom he wishes. Words like "we" and "they" acquire both intellectual and emotive meanings. The whole texture of the poetry is tightened as well as clarified as a result of Auden's having translated that vague feeling of being involved in transition into concrete terms: the poet fixing his attitude by addressing his younger contemporaries in the light of what the past was and what the future must be made to be. If he turns to address one of his own generation, such as Christopher Isherwood, he still carries with him the confidence he won in fixing his own attitude and ideal audience. We can see now how *The Orators* served as a training ground. Even when addressing the "Lords of limit," it is for his pupils' sake:

> Oldest of masters, whom the schoolboy fears
> Failing to find his pen, to keep back tears. . . . .

At the end of my corridor are boys who dream
Of a new bicycle or winning team;
On their behalf guard all the more
This late-maturing Northern shore,
Who to their serious season must shortly come.

That he is no longer between two stools, but living in a clearly apprehended moment of history, he makes clear in his poem to Isherwood:

This then my birthday wish for you, as now
From the narrow window of my fourth floor room
I smoke into the night, and watch reflections
Stretch into the harbour. In the houses
The little pianos are closed, and a clock strikes.
And all sway forward on the dangerous flood
Of history, that never sleeps or dies,
And, held one moment, burns the hand.

Though this is to a friend, there is no private symbolism, no fear of "public faces in private places." Auden the schoolmaster perhaps has his pupils to thank for his solution of this problem.

There are other problems that he has solved in this volume. The problem presented by the relation between tradition and revolution, which we saw tackled by Day Lewis, was felt even more keenly by Auden. Indeed, that was one reason for the ambiguity of his imagery, for there were things in the enemy's camp that he loved and their emotional meaning for him was thus confused. But now he has reached a position where all that was desirable in the past can be carried forward into the future: "heir and ancestor" are reconciled. He can pause to look back on the past while seeing his present predicament, and the past falls into its place and is accepted:

Language of moderation cannot hide;
My sea is empty and the waves are rough:
Gone from the map the shore where childhood played
Tight-fisted as a peasant, eating love;
Lost in my wake the archipelago,
Islands of self through which I sailed all day,
Planting a pirate's flag, a generous boy;
And lost the way to action and to you.

Lost if I steer. Gale of desire may blow
Sailor and ship past the illusive reef,
And I yet land to celebrate with you
Birth of a natural order and of love;
With you enjoy the untransfigured scene,
My father down the garden in his gaiters,
My mother at her bureau writing letters,
Free to our favours, all our titles gone.

This poise is a technical accomplishment; it does not mean that all the poems in this volume are optimistic or cheerful. The grim futility of "Casino" and the terror of poem No. VI are sufficient to disprove that. It is assurance of expression that Auden has achieved, and a synthesized point of view from which to praise or blame, accept or reject.

In February, 1940, there appeared *Another Time*, a collection of poems written by Auden mostly between 1937 and 1939. This volume, published by Random House, was the first book of poems by Auden to be published in America before it was published in Britain. For by this time Auden had crossed the Atlantic and settled in the United States. The poems of this collection seem to indicate some temporary falling-off of poetic power, and this may be directly related to the poet's changed situation. In a sense, Auden had to begin his poetic career all over again on settling in the United States. He had finally made up his mind about

England—and it had taken him a long time to do it; he had achieved a synthesis of his conflicting ideas, an audience to speak to, a symbolism that he could handle with confidence. And now the world was changing once again, and he had changed with it: he had to find a new pattern, a new audience, a new confidence.

Many of the poems in *Another Time* thus represent a transitional phase in Auden's career. He has changed his mind and his place as a man, and this reacts on his position as a poet. It looks as though the amount of competent but trivial verse in this volume is the result of his marking time while he looks for a new eminence from which to survey—not England this time but the world. In changing his status from British citizen to citizen of the world, he has revived some of his old problems, and he must wait for the new synthesis before he can write impressive serious poetry again:

> All mankind, I fancy,
> When anticipating
> Anything exciting
>   Like a rendez-vous,
>
> Occupy the time in
> Purely random thinking,
> For when love is waiting
>   Logic will not do. . . . .
>
> So I pass the time, dear,
> Till I see you, writing
> Down whatever nonsense
>   Comes into my head.

This poem of his own provides an interesting unconscious analogy. The "you" of the poem does not stand for Auden's new vantage point from which to get a unified view of the world, yet it might well do so.

There are some pleasing "occasional" poems in *Another Time*, but all the more serious verses—even "Spain," which was written in 1936—show a certain lack of integration. There is certainly no indication of any poetic progress since the publication of *On This Island*. Yet Auden could afford to mark time: his earlier work had given him a reputation as one of the most distinguished of the contemporary poets.

Stephen Spender, born in 1909, is the third and youngest of this trio of English poets that was hailed in 1934 as constituting a "hope for poetry." His first volume, *Poems* (1933), is a series of lyrical statements of personal situations out of which gradually emerges the suggestion of the necessity of change for England:

> oh young men oh young comrades
> it is too late now to stay in those houses
> your fathers built where they built you to build to breed
> money on money. . . . .

But many of the poems are simply explorations of his own attitudes and sensibility. He is less eager than Auden or Day Lewis to state his experiences in universal terms, and so we do not see in his poetry the same problem of symbols and audience that we get in the other two. He is content to take his images from what he sees and to express his ideas as they come. His verse has a smoothness, a limpid quality, that distinguishes it from that of his contemporaries. Perhaps he rated the poet's function less highly, for he did not try to force his experiences into inclusive patterns, into symbols of some urgent present reality. This makes his poetry easier to read, but less interesting, or at least less exciting. Some of his descriptive poetry possesses a grace

and control lacking entirely in the early work of Day
Lewis and Auden:

> More beautiful and soft than any moth
> With burring furred antennae feeling its huge path
> Through dusk, the air-liner with shut-off engines
> Glides over suburbs and the sleeves set trailing tall
> To point the wind. Gently, broadly, she falls
> Scarcely disturbing charted currents of air.

And we may quote the final verse of the same poem,
where description is effectively used as comment:

> Then, as they land, they hear the tolling bell
> Reaching across the landscape of hysteria
> To where, larger than all the charcoaled batteries
> And imaged towers against that dying sky,
> Religion stands, the church blocking the sun.

This poetry is so much quieter than Auden's; the poet
does not seem to consider himself so important.

We do find, however, though expressed in a more
subdued manner, the same themes that occupied Day
Lewis and Auden. The search for ancestors, the reconciliation of tradition and revolution, is to be seen here
too:

> I think continually of those who were truly great.
> Who, from the womb, remembered the soul's history
> Through corridors of light where the hours are suns
> Endless and singing. . . . .
>
> What is precious is never to forget
> The essential delight of the blood drawn from ageless springs
> Breaking through rocks in worlds before our earth.

A noteworthy feature of Spender's poetry is the success
with which he domiciles in his poetry imagery taken
from the modern industrial scene. His poem "The Express" will remain a classic, as one of the earliest suc-

cessful uses of such imagery in a perfectly natural manner.

The lack of obscurity in the poems of this volume is due partly to a natural tendency on Spender's part to quietness and simplicity in his poetry, partly to a deliberate avoidance of symbolization, a preference for comment through description rather than through fable. He gained to some extent freedom from the contemporary problem by limitation, by poetic humility. Thus he never writes as bad poetry as Auden can do, yet he has not the richness and excitement of Auden at his best.

His next publication was *Vienna* (1934), a long poem inspired by the notorious attack by the Austrian government under Dollfuss on the Viennese workers in their own quarters in May, 1934. Because of his refusal to use myth or fable, Spender had to depend on the sheer force of his statement in this poem, and as a result it does not quite come off. There is insufficient power and implication; some symbolizing device was really necessary to give richness and depth. Description, discussion, and argument are not enough, no matter how effective the verse in which they are expressed. By not employing the Audenesque type of myth, Spender saved himself from Auden's obscurity, but at the expense of a certain impoverishment.

The Trial of a Judge, "a tragic statement in five acts," written for the Group Theatre, appeared in 1938. By this time Spender's position as a popular-front communist was quite clear, both to himself and to others, and he had explained it in prose, notably in *Forward from Liberalism*. Thus he had an audience who thought generally in his terms and who spoke his language. *The Trial of a Judge* is an impressive account of the liberal in the hands of the conquering fascist, both a psychological study and a political allegory. The verse is simple, the language is straightforward and effective, and the play as a whole is a moving statement of a tragic modern situation. The basis of Spender's communism was really a humanitarian liberalism, and it is this that sets the frame of reference within which the story is told. There are no special sciences used for interpretation; the symbols are taken from contemporary history interpreted in the light of a simple yet urgent humanity. The play is one of the many examples of the simple and impressive literature produced by left-wing intellectuals (and nonintellectuals, if one may use the term) under the pressure of political events. The Franco rebellion in Spain helped very largely in stimulating this literature, as is witnessed by the collection of *Poems for Spain* edited by Spender and John Lehmann in 1939.

The Still Centre (1939) was Spender's next collection of poems. This volume includes everything he had written since the publication of the 1934 collection, and most of the poems had appeared in periodicals during the period. One or two have been re-written. The lyrical note of the earlier volume is sounded here with real distinction, though the poems are by no means uniform in quality. In his Foreword he lays his finger on one of the characteristics that distinguish him from his contemporary poets:

I have printed the Third Part separately . . . . because all these poems are concerned with the Spanish War. As I have decidedly supported one side—the Republican—in that conflict, perhaps I should explain why I do not strike a more heroic note. My reason is that a poet can only write about what is true to his own experience, not about what he would like to be true to his experience.

Poetry does not state truth, it states the conditions within which something felt is true. . . . . I think that there is a certain pressure of external events on poets today, making them tend to write about what is outside their own limited experience. The violence of the times we are living in, the necessity of sweeping and general and immediate action, tend to dwarf the experience of the individual. . . . . For this reason, in my most recent poems, I have deliberately turned back to a kind of writing which is more personal, and I have included within my subjects weakness and fantasy and illusion.

The vein of lyrical speculation in this volume sometimes produces poetry which can hold its own with anything produced in the century. "An Elementary School Class Room in a Slum" (one of the poems he re-wrote) is an example:

> All of their time and space are foggy slum
> So blot their maps with slums as big as doom.

> Unless, governor, teacher, inspector, visitor,
> This map becomes their window and these windows
> That open on their lives like crouching tombs
> Break, O break open, till they break the town
> And show the children to the fields and all their world
> Azure on their sands, to let their tongues
> Run naked into books, the white and green leaves open
> The history theirs whose language is the sun.

Spender was the one poet of this group who clung to his own experience, who did not seek patterns from thinkers or remedies from doctors, but sought to interpret himself in the light of his common humanity, and to interpret humanity in the light of himself. It so happened that he was sufficiently a personality, that his own experience was rich enough and right enough, for this interpretation to be an adequate basis for lyric poetry. Politically, he reached a position similar to that of his contemporary poets; poetically he remained apart, a poet who expressed as simply as he could the world's impingement on himself, rather than one who tried to construct a pattern of the world as it was apart from him yet using personal symbols in constructing the pattern. His own way is vindicated in such poems as "Ultima ratio regum":

> The guns spell money's ultimate reason
> In letters of lead on the spring hillside.
> But the boy lying dead under the olive trees
> Was too young and too silly
> To have been notable to their important eye.
> He was a better target for a kiss. . . . .
>
> Consider his life which was valueless
> In terms of employment, hotel ledgers, news files.
> Consider. One bullet in ten thousand kills a man.
> Ask. Was so much expenditure justified
> On the death of one so young and so silly
> Lying under the olive trees, O world, O death?

Spender's great virtue remains his lyrical simplicity, his directness, as Auden's is his exciting ambiguity, precarious balance amid opposites. They represent complementary aspects of the poet in the 1930's.

There were other poets in the 1930's, some, like Louis Macneice, good poets, whose work one might profitably discuss, but without adding any new insights into the nature of modern poetry. Not that Macneice does not possess an individual style—the difference between his manner and Auden's is reminiscent of that between the dull, peaty taste of Irish whisky and the wilder taste of Scotch—but the main types of situation existing between the poet and the modern world have been indicated, and further discussion, though welcome to the writer, would weary the reader, for it would involve much repetition. So we conclude this discussion, addressing to the reader Macneice's words to Auden:

> Our prerogatives as men
> Will be cancelled who knows when;
> Still I drink your health before
> The gun-butt raps upon the door.

EPILOGUE

POETRY is more important than the individual great poets, and perhaps it is a mistake to discuss it in terms of well-known names. At any rate, in singling out a group of poets for discussion, we have found it difficult not to obscure some significant facts about poetry—facts which have nothing to do with these distinguished poets but which are concerned with the anonymous people with whom poetry began. The tendency which began in the 1930's to write group poetry, to publish in anthologies, to express aspects of the contemporary social scene in direct and simple terms with the underlying expectation of change—this popular reaction to the pressure of political and economic events can too easily be overlooked. But popular poetry is always important, even if it is not good poetry. To record the names—when they are available—of those who have contributed to the development would serve little purpose, for its importance lies in its essential anonymity, its social feeling and group optimism. Some of it is slogan poetry, which upsets the sophisticated, and some is sentimental. A lot of it is very bad. But it shows the beginning of a new audience for poetry coincident with the decay of the pessimism of the 1920's and the rise of a fighting optimism which, paradoxically, was produced by the growing threat of fascism. A new unity, a new common symbolism, became possible between poet and public. This was the movement which the second World War overwhelmed. Whether it will emerge again and contribute something valuable to English poetry remains to be seen: but one is tempted to prophesy that it will, and that the struggle for Spain against the fascist invader, which gave the first real impetus to this movement, will one day be seen to have meant more for English poetry than the Greek struggle for independence meant for the Romantics of the early nineteenth century.

There are other things that might have been said. In particular, we should have liked to discuss the problems of the Scottish poet in the modern world, and in this connection to pay a much overdue tribute to that fine Scots poet "Hugh MacDiarmid" (C. M. Grieve). But in a book intended primarily for an American audience one must beware of introducing interests which, however important they might be on one side of the Atlantic, arouse (if undeservedly) less interest on the other. This book represents a compromise between what the writer wants to discuss and what he thinks his readers will be willing to read.

Poetry is the expression of men's mental and emotional experiences in the most direct and memorable manner. Any more limited definition would be pedantic, for it would be bound to exclude some verse which had significance for disciplined and sensitive readers. If poetry has a single function, it is to remind men of their humanity by increasing it; to present experiences which by their content bring recognition and by their form bring illumination. To touch as many significant truths as possible while nominally presenting a single subject, to name one letter of the alphabet in such a way that all the other letters will sing in joint and several implication—that is the function of technique in poetry. If we forget these things, as many of us in our criticism are inclined to do, we forget the sole *raison d'être* of our critical activity and so become helpless in face of the enemy.

In times like the present it becomes more and more imperative that we should understand why we consider literature to be important. There is no point in howling that culture is threatened if we can show no reason why it ought to be preserved. We must understand that the importance of the arts is bound up with the importance of life, that art means something only because human life means something, and that the forces which produce suffering and death on the physical level also produce corruption in art. We do not need to divide man into a political and an aesthetic animal, and that is fortunate, for few could survive the operation. No culture can be defended by those who have lost sight of the whole man.

Most critics are preachers *manqués*. We all like to see our readers share our general views about art and life, and at the slightest excuse we become grandiloquent. Sometimes we comfort ourselves with the thought that a careful criticism will communicate its own assumptions. But we are all at the mercy of our interpreters, all critics from Aristotle down to the meanest columnist that blows, and no postscript put in as an insurance against misunderstanding has ever been read in the spirit in which it was written. As the critic writes his final line, with a mixture of relief and regret, he feels that in spite of everything he has left his most urgent argument unsaid.

INDEX

Abbey Theatre, 141, 162
Abbott, C. C., 9, 25, 27
Achievement of T. S. Eliot, The, 122
L'Action française, 93
"Adam's Curse," 158–59
"Address for a Prize-Day," 221
Æ; *see* Russell, George
After Strange Gods, 91
Aldington, Richard, 79, 82, 83, 84, 85, 99
Allingham, William, 137
"Anashuya and Vijaya," 136
Another Time, 231–33
"Anthem for Doomed Youth," 69, 70
"Argument," 223
Arnold, Matthew, 6, 23, 75
"Ash Wednesday," 126
Auden, W. H., 1, 4, 35, 36, 153, 190, 192, 194, 195, 200, 203, 205, 206, 209, 214–33, 234, 238, 239
Autobiography of William Butler Yeats, 129, 138, 178

Babbitt, Irving, 93, 94
Baillie, A. W. M., 27
Bards of the Gael and Gall, 138
"Battalion in Rest," 64
Battle, 62
Beardsley, Aubrey, 11, 89
Belloc, Hilaire, 73
Bergson, Henri, 93
Bible, the, 123
Blake, William, 52, 133, 135, 142, 148, 155
Blunden, Edmund, 45, 56, 64–65
Boehme, Jacob, 133, 147
Borderlands, 47
Bottomley, Gordon, 45–46
Bridges, Robert, 22–23, 25, 26, 28, 32, 33, 35, 192
"Broken Dreams," 163
Brooke, Rupert, 41, 42, 59–60
Browne, Sir Thomas, 104
Browning, Robert, 4, 5, 6, 7, 14, 18, 108

Burke, Kenneth, 174
Burns, Robert, 150
"Byzantium," 180, 181–85

Campbell, Roy, 90
Carpenter, Edward, 35
Cathay, 78
Celtic Twilight, The, 146
Chaucer, Geoffrey, 49, 82
Chesterton, G. K., 73
"Coat, A," 166
"Cold Heaven, The," 166
Coleridge, S. T., 39, 180
"Coming of Wisdom with Time, The," 162
"Conflict, The," 206
"Consecration, A," 48
Corbière, Tristan, 116
Counter-attack, 63
Crabbe, George, 47, 50
"Cramped in That Funnelled Hole," 66
Crossways, 145
Cunard, Nancy, 86
Cutting of an Agate, The, 156

Daffodil Fields, The, 49
Daily Bread, 47
Dance of Death, The, 227–28
Dante, 113, 118, 125
Dauber, 49
Davidson, John, 139
Davies, W. H., 45, 53–54
Day Lewis, Cecil, 35, 192–213, 227, 230, 233, 234
De la Mare, Walter, 43, 111, 112
Des Imagistes: An Anthology, 83
Destructive Element, The, 224–26
"Disabled," 68
"Discovery," 57
"Disenchantment," 87
Disraeli, Benjamin, 9
Dixon, R. W., 25
Dobson, Austin, 22

Donne, John, 5, 29, 30, 34, 37, 53, 56, 104, 105, 115, 175, 192
Doolittle, Hilda, 79, 80, 82, 83, 84, 99, 100, 101
Dowson, Ernest, 11, 13, 139, 164
Dramatis Personae, 159, 160
Drinkwater, John, 44
Dryden, John, 29
Dynasts, The, 18

Earthly Paradise, The, 7
"East Coker," 103
"Easter, 1916," 176–77
Egoist, the, 82–83
"Elementary School Class Room in a Slum, An," 237
Eliot, T. S., 83, 85, 86, 91, 93, 94, 96, 97, 99–105, 106–27, 128, 129, 131, 153, 190, 192, 193, 196, 214
Ellis, Edwin, 148
Elton, Oliver, 5
Epstein, Jacob, 92
Everlasting Mercy, The, 49
"Everlasting Voices, The," 154
"Exposure," 66
"Express, The," 234–35

"Farm near Zillebeke, A," 64
"February 1936," 210
Ferguson, Sir Samuel, 137
"Few Don'ts by an Imagiste, A," 82
Fires, 47, 48
Fletcher, John Gould, 78, 83, 84, 99
Flint, F. S., 81, 82, 83
Foerster, Norman, 94
Fool i' the Forest, A, 85
Forward from Liberalism, 235
Frazer, Sir James, 120
Freeman, John, 44, 57–58, 61
Freud, Sigmund, 214
From Feathers to Iron, 195, 199–201
From Ritual to Romance, 120
Frost, Robert, 71
Further Letters of Gerard Manley Hopkins, 9, 27

"Gallows, The," 71
Gautier, Théopile, 82
Georgian poetry; *see* Georgian poets
Georgian Poetry, 1911–1912, 38

Georgian Poetry, 1916–1917, 61
Georgian poets, 9, 22, 23, 37, 38–60, 61, 62, 64, 66, 70, 71, 72, 74, 75, 86, 96, 102, 107, 110, 111
"Gerontion," 114
Gibson, Wilfrid Wilson, 43, 47–48, 49, 50, 61, 62, 64
Golden Bough, The, 120
Green Helmet and Other Poems, The, 155, 157, 158, 161, 163
Gregory, Lady, 138, 141, 160, 162
Grierson, Sir Herbert, 175
Grieve, C. M., 241
Group Theatre, 235

H.D.; *see* Doolittle, Hilda
"Happy Is England Now," 57, 61
Hardy, Thomas, 17–18, 19
"Hare, The," 48
"Haystack in the Floods, The," 7
Hedges, L. P., 206
Heine, Heinrich, 82
Henley, W. E., 22
Herbert, George, 105, 115
Hesiod, 117
"Hippopotamus, The," 114
History of Ireland, Heroic Period, 138, 143
"Hollow Men, The," 124–25
Homer, 118, 119
Hope for Poetry, A, 192, 194–95, 196
Hopkins, Gerard Manley, 9, 24–35, 37, 53, 192, 214, 219
"Hosting of the Sidhe, The," 153
Housman, A. E., 19–21
Hughes, Glenn, 74
Hulme, T. E., 74–75, 76–79, 81, 90–99, 105
Huxley, Aldous, 87
Huxley, Thomas, 129, 132
Hyde, Douglas, 139

Ideas of Good and Evil, 138, 148, 149, 150, 151, 152
Imagism; *see* Imagists
Imagist Anthology, 1930, 84
Imagists, 53, 73–85, 86, 96, 98, 99, 102, 105, 107
"In Memory of Major Robert Gregory," 163

"In the Heart of Contemplation," 210

In Memoriam, 4, 29

In the Seven Woods, 155, 157, 158

"Indian to His Love, The," 136

"Into the Twilight," 154

Irish Literary Society, the, 141

Isherwood, Christopher, 229

Island of Statues, The, 137

Isle Adam, Villiers de l', 147

"It Was the Lovely Moon," 57

Johnson, Lionel, 11, 13, 139, 164

"Journal of an Airman," 221, 224, 225–26

Joyce, James, 21, 83, 102

Keats, John, 14, 16, 27

Kipling, Rudyard, 22, 36

"La Figlia che piange," 114

Laforgue, Jules, 116

"Lament," 61

Landor, Walter Savage, 164

"Landscapes," 99

Lang, Andrew, 22

Last Poems (Housman), 20

Last Poems (Yeats), 188–89

Last Poems and Plays, 171

Lawrence, D. H., 35, 51–53, 82–83, 84

Lawrence, T. E., 225

Ledwidge, Francis, 44, 71

Le Gallienne, Richard, 139

Lehmann, John, 236

"Letter to a Wound," 224–25

Letters of Gerard Manley Hopkins to Robert Bridges, The, 25, 30, 35

Lewis, Cecil Day; *see* Day Lewis, Cecil

Livelihood, 47

Look, Stranger, 228–31

"Love Song of J. Alfred Prufrock, The," 101, 113–14, 117

Love Songs of Connacht, 139

Lowell, Amy, 82, 83, 84, 85

Lustra, 78

Lycidas, 122

"Lyonesse," 18

Lyrical Ballads, 39

"MacDiarmid, Hugh," 241

"Macleod, Fiona"; *see* Sharp, William

Macneice, Louis, 171, 188, 238, 239

Maeterlinck, Maurice, 147

"Magi, The," 166

Magnetic Mountain, The, 195, 201–5, 212

Mallarmé, Stéphane, 13, 79 147,

"Man Who Dreamed of Faeryland, The," 144

Manilius, 20

"Marina," 126

"Market Girl, The", 18

Marsh, Edward, 38, 40, 46, 58

Marx, Karl, 214, 228

Masefield, John, 48–51

Mathers, Macgregor, 131

Matthiessen, F. O., 122

Melville, Herman, 198

"Mental Cases," 68

Meynell, Alice, 9, 11

"Michael," 50

Michael Robartes and the Dancer, 168, 174, 176–77

Milton, John, 122, 123

Monro, Harold, 45

Monroe, Harriet, 79

Montaigne, Michel, Comte de, 94, 96, 97

Moore, T. Sturge, 46

More, Paul Elmer, 93

Morris, William, 7, 8

"Mosada," 27

"Mountain Tomb, The," 166

"Mr. Apollinax," 114

"Mr. Epstein and the Critics," 92

"Music Comes," 57

"Nabara, The," 211–12

National Literary Society, the, 141

"Never Give All the Heart," 159

New Age, 92

New Poems (Yeats), 188

Newbolt, Henry, 22

Noah and the Waters, 209, 212

Notebook of Malte Laurids Brigge, 224

Note-Books and Papers of Gerard Manley Hopkins, The, 27

"November Skies," 57

O'Grady, Standish, 138, 143
Old Huntsman, The, 63
"Old Men Admiring Themselves in the Water, The," 159
"Old Vicarage, Grantchester, The," 41
On This Island, 228–31
Orators, The, 194, 219–27, 229
Overtures to Death and Other Poems, 209–13
Owen, Wilfred, 65–70, 71, 192, 201, 214

Paid on Both Sides, 215
Parnell, C. S., 140
Pascal, Blaise, 94, 96, 98
Patmore, Coventry, 8, 9, 25, 27
"Phases of the Moon, The," 169
"Pigeons, The," 57
Plotinus, 185, 187
Poems (W. H. Auden) 214–19
Poems and Ballads of Young Ireland, 39
Poems for Spain, 236
Poems of Wilfred Owen, The, 66
Poetry: A Magazine of Verse, 79, 80
Poets and Poetry of Munster, 138
Pope, Alexander, 53
"Portrait of a Lady," 114
Pound, Ezra, 77–78, 80, 81, 82, 83, 85, 109, 118
"Prayer for My Daughter, A," 163
"Preludes," 99
Pre-Raphaelites, 6, 10, 46, 136, 139–40, 155
Prior, Matthew, 164
Propertius, 20

"Red Hanrahan's Song about Ireland," 158
Reflections on Violence, 91
Responsibilities, 163–67
Revolution in Writing, 209
Reynard the Fox, 49
"Rhapsody on a Windy Night," 114
Rhymers' Club, 13, 14, 17, 139
Richards, I. A., 102
Rilke, Rainer Maria, 224, 225
Rimbaud, Arthur, 13, 116
Riposte, 76, 77, 78

Rolleston, T. W., 139
Rose, The, 142, 144, 145, 146, 147, 152
"Rose of the World, The," 143
Rosenberg, Isaac, 71
Rossetti, D. G., 6, 7, 84, 135, 164
Rousseau, Jean Jacques, 92, 94
"Rural Economy (1917)," 64
Russell, George, 142

"Sailing to Byzantium," 180, 181, 182, 184
Sassoon, Siegfried, 58, 61, 62–64, 68, 88
Secret Rose, The, 148
"Self-criticism and Answer," 212
"Sentry's Mistake, The," 64
Shakespeare, William, 16, 53, 119
Shelley, P. B., 1, 14, 23, 84, 135, 136, 137, 140, 142, 155, 164
Shropshire Lad, A, 20
Sigerson, George, 138
Sitwell, Edith, 86, 88, 89
Sitwell, Osbert, 87, 88, 90
Sitwell, Sacheverell, 88
"Six Odes," 221, 226–27
Skeleton, John, 214
"Snap-Dragon," 51
"Song of the Old Mother, The," 154
Sorel, Georges, 91, 92, 93
"Spain," 233
Speculations, 93, 94
Spender, Stephen, 1, 192, 194, 205, 220, 224, 233–38
Spenser, Edmund, 23, 135, 136, 137, 142
"Statement," 224
Stein, Gertrude, 89, 90
Stevenson, R. L., 22
Still Centre, The, 236–38
"Stolen Child, The," 136
"Stone Trees," 57
"Strange Meeting," 70
Swedenborg, Emanuel, 133, 147
"Sweeney Erect," 114
"Sweetheart, Do Not Love Too Long," 159
"Symbolism in Painting," 150
"Symbolism of Poetry, The," 150

INDEX

Symbolists, French, 81, 88, 112, 113, 139, 147, 192
Swinburne, Algernon Charles, 8
Symons, Arthur, 13

Tables of the Law, The, 148
"Tears," 72
Tennyson, Alfred, 4, 5, 6, 7, 10, 13, 14, 17, 18, 19, 21, 24, 26, 27, 29, 31, 32, 36, 53, 108, 152
Thomas, Edward, 71–72
Thompson, Francis, 9, 11
Thoroughfares, 47
Time To Dance and Other Poems, A, 205–9
Tithonus, 5
"To a Poet Who Would Have Me Praise Certain Bad Poets," 162
"To a Shade," 165–66
"To an Isle in the Water," 136
"To Ireland in the Coming Times," 147
Todhunter, John, 139
"Tom's Garland," 32
Tottel's Miscellany, 39
Tower, The, 146, 168, 174, 179–81, 186
"Tower, The," 163
"Tradition and the Individual Talent," 118
Transitional Poem, 195, 196–99, 200, 201, 203, 205, 212
Tree, Iris, 87
Trembling of the Veil, The, 131, 141
Trial of a Judge, The, 235–36
Triple Thinkers, The, 21
Turner, W. J., 42
"Twentieth Century Harlequinade," 87
Tyndall, John, 129, 132

"Ultima ratio regum," 238
Ulysses, 102
"Unappeasable Host, The," 154

Upanishads, 120
"Upon a House Shaken by the Land Agitation," 162

Verlaine, Paul, 13, 116, 147, 157
"Verses, Translations, and Reflections from 'The Anthology,' " 80
Vienna, 235
Villon, François, 82
Vision, A, 170
"Vlamertinghe: Passing the Chateau, July 1917," 64

Walpole, Horace, 58
Wanderings of Oisin, The, 136–37
Wanderings of Usheen, The; see *Wanderings of Oisin, The*
Warner, Rex, 203, 209, 221
Waste Land, The, 85, 96, 102, 103, 117, 120–24
Weston, Jessie L., 120, 123
Wheels, 86, 87
Wheels and Butterflies, 187
Whitman, Walt, 34–35, 37
Widow in the Bye Street, The, 49
Wild Swans at Coole, The, 168–69, 174–76
Wilde, Oscar, 8
Wilson, Edmund, 21
Wind among the Reeds, The, 147, 151–55
Winding Stair, The, 146, 168, 174, 179–85, 186
Wolfe, Humbert, 88, 90
"Woman Young and Old, A," 187
"Words for Music Perhaps," 131, 187
Wordsworth, William, 1, 4, 12, 39, 53, 55, 56
Works and Days, 117
Worringer, Wilhelm, 78–79

Yeats, William Butler, 1, 27, 128–55, 156–89, 190, 193, 196, 213, 220, 221